The Monographs

Becoming Sherlock Holmes

2nd Edition

Ben Cardall

Hardcover ISBN 978-1-80424-416-6
Paperback ISBN 978-1-80424-417-3
ePub ISBN 978-1-80424-418-0
PDF ISBN 978-1-80424-419-7

Published by MX Publishing
335 Princess Park Manor, Royal Drive,
London, N11 3GX
www.mxpublishing.co.uk

Cover design by Awan

Cookie - Cookster - My Boy

None of this would be possible without you

I love you buddy

Foreword

Hello reader! First of all, thank you for taking the time to read this book, for the ones who've been following its progress you'll know it's been made with a labour of love by Ben. Second, to tell you about my connection to its author and the amazing work that he does, which leads to my third point; why you've made a wise decision to purchase the Monographs 2.0!

I met Ben around about a decade ago now, and to call me naive to the world of mentalism when we were introduced would be a gargantuan understatement, bringing to light the elephant in the room here...who the hell am I to help introduce you to his work?! Well, within the years that I have been working with Ben, I've had the pleasure of filming and editing a variety of projects that incorporate his methods on an entertaining platform, during which I learnt that these skills weren't just spectacle assets to his performance as an entertainer, but they could actually be applied to life as a whole. Like what a lot of people would naturally do when meeting someone like Ben, I probed for demonstrations. While he was more than happy to comply, I never thought to ask about the information. What was behind the veil? How did he accomplish such illusion? "Well, observation." You'll be surprised how much of a pause I left after he stated one of the key components to achieving these techniques, mainly because I wasn't actually expecting him to give away the trick! Of course, it obviously wasn't a trick, and this clearly was just the tip of the iceberg. It's funny how your brain expects more elusive solutions. And that's the key realisation to Ben's methods, they're not elusive. They're actually accessible, adaptable and of course do-able! I've witnessed this first hand, whether it be in his deductive experiments, our Web Series 'The Deductionist, or via the content he provides online! The courses he's ran have gone deeper within this (as I'm sure his students will tell you!), and make you wonder how far the rabbit hole really goes (points for the film reference!). Let's talk about the Monographs though, because that's why you're here! A handbook like no other for those wanting to dive into the field of people reading, observation and memorisation. When Ben first told me about its first edition, I was in awe that he'd managed to condense his wisdom into a product that would allow people to learn these skills for themselves! A lot of material we created heavily used these techniques and I knew Ben was already thinking about how he could take it further, ideas were already floating around as he was exploring new ways of applying them to his everyday life. I knew he wanted to ensure that these could work if brought to the table, there was no room to provide something without meaning, he wanted to create something that could be of use to everyone.

And now here we are, a long time coming and I'm sure the works paid off because you now have in your hands not just a great book, but a tool that will help guide you in whatever field your pursuit is in, because it's practically a universal tool! It's also one that I've seen in action. I've seen the benefits of it for Ben and others he's taught. I've seen the profound way it's changed perspective of those who've used the knowledge provided within these very pages. In our web series, you'll see for yourselves how Ben uses these methods himself in a practical and realistic fashion. Yes it's obviously done in a way to entertain and channel his Sherlockian vibe for the show, but it's also meant to enlighten viewers and adjust their ideas of what these skills can look like in the real world compared to the amplified nature of them in other media.

Ben's teachings will challenge you, but in the right way. That's why we challenge ourselves, to benefit from the result. Believe me, you will benefit from the results you gain from the Monographs. So stop hanging around this foreword and move forward (High five for the word play? No? Anyone?) with your journey into The Monographs! You're in safe hands with Ben's work, it's a process like no other and there's nothing else out there (save for the first edition!) that I've seen go so in depth into these methods. Now, off down the rabbit hole with you!

Adam

Prologue

Here we are then everybody, a second edition! Is that a daunting prospect? Sure. Is it going to be something that is worthwhile, needed, and going to up the ante on your work, day in and day out? Absolutely it is!

2014 is when I completed the final draft of the first edition and since that time my world has changed completely and for the better. Since that time I have worked more and more in the private sector field of security, taking cases, remote assessments, corporate espionage, interviewing and the list goes on and on and on. These are opportunities that are laid at the feet of the first round of The Monographs in total and complete gratitude. I would love for each and every one of you to check out my training platform and get involved - Omniscient-insights.com. I am now one of the Directors at Procypher Protective Services and run my own Executive protection and Investigations business - Integris Solutions and have taken numerous private sector cases and assessments in the security/Ep world. Stepping into the world of elite level coaching for corporations, security teams and military factions around the world as well. Even teaching one or two of the big names in the field a thing or two, but that will be a mystery for you to solve. Why am I telling you all this? Because I need my ego stroked?....maybe a little, but the more important aspect of this is that since this first edition was released, I have worked on this material day in and day out for 10 years. I have matured in my understanding of what works and what doesn't in the 'real world'.

It is one thing to be able to look at someone in a particular setting and have a complete idea of what this information is that is being communicated to you. It is quite another to be able to be aware of the many variables that occur from a single observation and be able to track them all as your conversation or interaction with a particular situation moves forward. The first edition broke new ground in terms of collecting information under one roof that can be used by the modern day observer of Non Verbal Communication (One thing that hasn't changed in all these years is that I still don't care what I am called. Whether that be a Deductionist or anything else) so now with the second edition, what is it that I would be looking to add? Why do I feel that you will get just as much from this as you did from the first? The answer is inherently a simple one, comprehension.

For those of you out there in the wilderness that have ever taken a martial arts class, you will be painfully aware of the benefits that understanding what doesn't work in a scenario can bring. After all, you can't have the yin without the yang right? As such your comprehension and grasp of this material is only going to grow. To see its transition and development is to know where this can be applied in your own day to day lives. Whether this be in your job, or at home or even in a bus queue. The application is what stops this book from being just a bunch of things that you know and helps it to become skills that can enhance yours and the lives of everyone you interact with. After all, you become the people that see things that nobody else can because either they don't want to or simply cannot be bothered. This comes with it a weight of responsibility. How are you going to use this?

For the most part, this will be a development of each of the chapters from the first edition. However there will be some of the work and some of the chapters that have been cut to make way for some of what I feel to be more important when it comes to matters of 'deduction'. In that way this is a second edition but it is also my hope that this can be viewed as a separate entity entirely.

I realise that almost nobody reads these parts of the books they buy but I wanted to use this to say a few thank-yous. There are many people who have helped me in my journey along the way. To those who have made my life difficult, thank you. You helped me to grow stronger and more determined with every passing day. To those that spoke of me in hushed tones and behind peoples backs, I am actually very grateful. You helped me to sharpen my state control in the face of everything my emotional qualities tried to tell me. The only man I will ever love, my brother from another species', Cookie. I know you will never read this, but I can read it to you. You have gotten me through most of my adult life and I couldn't ask for anyone better than you. Love you Buddy!

The John Watson to my Sherlock, Adam. My human brother from another mother! You are a special man sir! Here's to many more adventures in this world. My wife Maddie, the woman, my love. The support you have shown to my lunacy at times and smiling through the situations I get myself into even when I know you are scared for me. Thank you. I couldn't do any of this without you. Finally, and most importantly, you. Thank you to you for reading this and showing an interest in the development of these skills. Whether it be because you are fans of the incarnations, the podcast or just curiosity, thank you. It is because of you that this material gets tested and played with and new data discovered. You guys are quite simply the best!

Anyway, enough chatter! The game is afoot!

Developing Your Deductive Eye

'My mind is like a racing engine, tearing itself to pieces because it is not connected up with the work for which it was built. Life is commonplace'

The first time round we looked at the realisation of acquisition. The understanding that yes, these are fictional skills as Sherlock wields them by virtue of the fact that he is fictional (as much as it pains me to say). To some this gave the impression that what he could do was fictional as well. Once you understand where the sensationalised prospects pop up it becomes easier to see where one could develop training angles for 'real life'. In short, what this chapter will look to develop is one's mindset. This would be the concrete foundations upon which everything else is built. To that end, there are several matters that we can attend to in order to address this. From a training perspective, I take a very combative approach in using this. Making you ready for the things you will encounter in whichever vocation you are in. Once your mind is ready, you can then start to take these skills out for applications and use. You are after all, building cerebral skills and so you will need to make sure you are prepared for as many troubling aspects as you can be.

After all *'Emotional qualities are antagonistic to clear reasoning'* right? If I have said that once, I have said it a thousand times. Doesn't stop it being any less relevant. Heaven forbid you be working and interviewing someone over something important. They insult you and then because you have an emotional moment in response to this, you miss something vital in their non-verbals. For me this started with the Stoics of old and moved into a bunch of different disciplines. Aspects that are very easy to describe but a challenge to get to grips with. For example, I just mentioned the risk of missing details and yet the reality is that you will miss them. This is something that much like the certainly of our lives one day coming to an end, will happen. You are not the Terminator, capable of taking in very single tiny detail because of your overly developed CPU. How does someone who works in the world of observation accept that? Gaining control of your critical faculties. See, simple right? Doing it though is something else entirely. Take a look at these statements:

'You have power over your mind - not outside events. Realise this and you will find your strength' - Marcus Aurelius

'We should always be asking ourselves: "Is this something that is, or is not, in my control?' Epictetus

'How does it help...to make troubles heavier by bemoaning them?' - Seneca

I could cite these quite literally all day. The nature of emotional interference is something that we have all faced on a day to day basis. The simplest way that I had it explained to me was 'There are 2 types of problems in this world. Things you can solve and things you can't. So why would you worry about either of them?' That was an epiphany for me when I heard this.

If you have ever been arguing with someone, what do you think would happen if someone stopped the shouting for long enough to say ,"Why are we doing this?" Once you get past the 'well they think this and I think this of it all' it will boil down to words to the effect of 'Well I think I am right and I want them to acknowledge this'. That is not to say that arguments should never happen, they can be cathartic. I mention this more to highlight that the nature of the argument is for someone to deem themselves the winner. This provides no resolution to the point of the discussion anyway. There is a definitive cultural prospect to this in terms of emotional interference. For those who are familiar with the works of Lisa Feldman Barrett will know well that people develop their own view of an emotion and the actions it leads to as a result of their experience. Though we will look into that more in the coming chapters. How then, do we gain control, or at the very least channel the waves of actions that are connected to your emotions. What I am about to propose here is something that I developed and have used with every single one of my students over the years. So to be brutally honest, this doesn't come from laboratory conditions. However, this works and has done for some time.

I often think that I was predisposed towards emotional control or being overtly rational about certain things. The stories my mum tells me from when I was a kid as young as 5 or 6 asking my friends why they were crying in relation to something that had happened or a film that they watched. What is the point? I would ask, what do you get out of it? Rather than recount the misgivings of the 'professionals' I have encountered, I believe that this has helped me to create something practical in terms of developing control in this area. So, where do we start?

When I started to train my memory many years ago it was not to enter competitions or to put on demonstrations, it was to assist others and myself in whatever problem I was tasked to help with. It became abundantly clear very early on that the state of mind I was in had a direct effect on my ability to engage in the information I was looking at. I developed my memory along the same lines as fighters training for their next bout. I began referring to it as Combat memory.

If I am going to function in the best way possible in every scenario that I should encounter then I would need to have complete control over my mind. Complete control over that little voice that lives in your head that tells you things are one way, when in fact they are another. We can do this to a certain degree but as we are not actually robots, we won't hit that full T1000 capacity. I would ask yourself if you even wanted to. The analogous voice in your head is something those with Aphantasia can skip past.

When we look at memorization in terms of the aeons of playing cards or numbers that Mentathletes will sit down to, it is impressively tackled and yet it is almost always done in silence. Some people even go as far as to wear sound cancelling headphones and even blinkers to blot out the rest of the world so that they can concentrate. For those that wish to be observant to the same capacity as the titular

Holmes it is frequently impossible to be able to do this. So we have to develop our concentration using other means and it is the manipulation of the changes between brain waves states that can provide us with this.

The first research into the measurement of these began as far back as the 1930's when a German Scientist Hans Berger discovered Alpha Waves in Humans. Since then, the control of the changes between these states in relation to cognitive capacity has been tested and pushed in all manner of ways. During the early 2000's there was a craze that took over the UK in the form of the Nintendo DS and one of the extremely popular games involved 'Brain Training'. These games tested your ability to keep your brainwave state in alignment with the task you were doing and only became challenging when you started to misalign. It is something that 8 times world Memory Champion Dominic O'Brien makes use of as part of his training. Even using various machines to help him maintain his states of mind.

It is very often thought that the quicker you move, the quicker you think and therefore the more you are capable of doing. When it comes to the critical thought involved in memorising or any other related field like observing, the opposite is in fact true. As emotions can have a major say in the particular state of mind we are in and what we can deal with on a cerebral level, it would behove us to take as much control of the link between body and mind. This is an immutable link. If you were to force a smile on your face there is a neurological response. On a level that would be entirely dependent on you, there is a release of endorphins in relation to the response that is so known to you. In this case, smiling. You will get a release of dopamine, serotonin and endorphins. The more control we have, the more we are able to process. So let's take a look at the 5 most common states that we exist in. There are exceptions to this, such as Hyper-Gamma state but this comes with other side effects. Not only are most EEG's incapable of measuring this but when you are processing at close to 100 Hz then this would mean that you are more than likely missing details from the 'real world' as Hyper-Gamma waves are directly related to matters of intense concentration. The following are the most common states:

BETA - 14-25 hz - High level of mental activity. Associated with decision making, logic and problem solving. Decisions that are made at the kind of speed that snapping your fingers would be made at.

SMR - 12-14 hz - This stands for Sensorimotor Rhythm and while this is technically information that you don't really need to understand it, it does provide you with measurable details to memorise this. This state benefits a quiet body, active mind, attention, sequencing, information storage, retrieval. Ideal for sports - when you see fighters pacing around their dressing room warming up with punches and some light pad work, this is the state of mind they are in.

ALPHA - 8-12 HZ - Relaxed but alert state of mind. Mindfulness operates from this state. Though for my own two pennies, I would actively encourage you to forget this ambiguous title of Mindfulness. To tell someone to practise Mindfulness and then provide no further information is a lot like telling water not to be wet.

THETA - 4-8 HZ - Optimal state of mind of health heightened creativity, Painters and writers operate from this state. It is the state of mind I am in right now.

DELTA - Less than 4 HZ - Deep physical and mental relaxation. That moment just before sleep is the most relatable example for the Delta state. Have you ever wondered why you seem to be thinking the most profound things at this moment?

Given that emotions directly affect states of mind which then in turn will directly affect your physicality. Can we therefore capitalise on this road in which information is communicated. If I can control my emotion and physicality, can I control my state of mind? That is the real crux of the matter. After all this time the answer is yes, but it is to a matter of degrees. You will never be able to switch from full belly laughter to calm (unless you are faking that is) by using these bio-feedback hacks. What you can do is to make sure that you are thinking as clearly as possible in all situations.

Think of it this way. You are completing your 9-5 on a busy Wednesday. You know that when you get in you have to go to the gym for your personal training session because you are trying to lose weight. The dogs also need to be walked and you have last night's dishes in the sink that need to be done. Around 4:30 it gets very busy. Phone calls, messages, people, noise, shouting, conversations, you're hungry and then just like that, you're done. You walk up to your front door, your feet hurt and you have given yourself a tension headache. Add to that the fact that it has been raining so you are now

7

also cold and wet. You open the front door and you are greeted by a wave of warmth due to the timing of your heating. You take your coat and shoes off and sit on the sofa to stroke your dogs. You sit back into the chair and breathe a sigh of relief. You look at your watch and your training session starts in 20 minutes. Ask yourself honestly, in this situation, are you going to the gym or are you cancelling? Let's face it, the most likely scenario is a missed session. Would this have been the same outcome if you had never sat down?

Now I am not here to argue the specific neurological turning points involved and the many variable possibilities but what comes out of the experience is something that you would struggle to refute. The different physical moments lead to different thoughts in relation to the next task. The motion of the ocean doesn't stop if you don't sit down. Think about this, if you are one of those people that snack when bored then why does having something else to do take your mind off the impending treat? Thoughts, actions, feelings are all intertwined so we need to develop a feedback sign as we shift between states so we can capitalise on changes as and when they occur. With there being around 8 billion of us on the planet at the time of writing this, the ability to prepare for all eventualities seems unlikely. Though we can prepare ourselves to face all situations.

There is a relatable yet problematic study that we can use to further understand this. It was the work of Neuroscientist Benjamin Libet in the 1980's. He had hooked his subjects up to an EEG to try and prove or disprove the legitimacy of free will. They were asked to flex a wrist, not to think about flexing a wrist and then flex but just to flex it. It was discovered that there was unconscious brain activity associated with the action, consistently. For an average of a half a second before the participants were aware of the decision to move, the activity could be monitored. This experiment appears to offer evidence of Wegner's view that decisions are first made by the brain, and there is a delay before we become conscious of them. It is debatable whether people are able to accurately record the moment of their decision to move. Our subjective awareness of decisions is very unreliable. This is where the experiment starts to become problematic.

What we can learn from this in relation to our emotions and the states that accompany them is that they have begun before we become aware of them. This leads to a physical expression of them. Not in a Darwinian, universality way but in a personal way. If we learn more about what our responses are then we can impede this proactively to stop things from becoming out of our control. For example, with myself when I get annoyed by something I tend to stretch out my fingers and clench my jaw so it looks like it is bubbling. My usual triggers are things like the music of Justin Bieber or the baffling longevity of Love Island. I get this familiar ache in my jaw and start to feel the stretching of my palm. For me to make sure that I am aware of as much information in the room as I can be I need to be there, be present in that moment. Not in a spiritual sense but if we are looking to give ourselves a process to develop awareness then this is invaluable. Once I start to get that throb in my mandible I am basically telling my brain that my fingers are in my ears. To stop this from becoming out of my control I can forcibly keep my palm from stretching and put my tongue between my teeth. Giving me the control I need to stay present and engaged in the information I am seeing.

To help you better understand the benefits that clarity in cognition can have to your ability to perform whatever it is that you have been tasked to do, I present this game. Are you all familiar with the Stroop test? Well on the off chance that you are not, the game would go like this. The Stroop effect being the delay in reaction time between congruent and incongruent stimuli. The Stroop test is designed to inhibit cognitive interference. We add into this our changing brain wave states and we have a training scenario that would replicate a 'real life' event. Information being fired at you that is outside of your control with a specific task blended with changing emotional states. It was Sherlock Holmes himself that taught us *'Emotional Qualities are antagonistic to clear reasoning'.*

The QR code will take you to a YouTube video for the stroop test. There are four rounds in this video. It begins with an explanation of

the game in terms of what you are required to do. I am adding an additional task to each round. In the first you just tap your feet, 1 at a time and don't stop until the end. For the second round, snap your fingers on any hand you choose and don't stop until the end. For the third round I want you to stop the physical actions with your hands and feet and just hold a fist with both hands, as tight as you can. For the final round I want you to do star jumps however only if it is safe and appropriate to do so. If you have any injuries then please just keep the fists going. This makes an already taxing event that much harder. Forcing that little voice that exists in your head to tell you the test is way harder than it actually is. We get control over this and everything we do or think about becomes immeasurably easier. However the real purpose of this is for you to understand how a change of state will affect how you process information cognitively.

What I would encourage you to do following on from this is to develop a behavioural inventory of sorts. In developing mine, I would take stock of as many different situations that I would encounter whilst in the 5 different brainwave states. This would be everything from standing in a queue to being in an argument. Here some examples for you to play with:

The Last Time You Felt Deep Fear - Are you freeze, flight, fight? Did you feel hot or cold? What did your heart rate do? What was the stigma? Does this change with repeated exposure? Are there varying levels? What was the weather like during the last time? Anything and everything. If you think it is irrelevant, add it anyway.

The Last Time You Exercised - Doesn't matter what it is, running upstairs to the toilet, dancing, the gym, sex anything. Does your heart race or do you sweat, or both? Does it smell? Does it change if it's cold? Does it change if it's in a different location? (I also realise that if you chose sex, there is hilarity that will ensue)

11

The Last Time You Stood In A Queue - Was it for transport, coffee, the bathroom, the supermarket? Were there many people? Was it a posh area? Any reprobates about? Any beautiful people? What could you smell? What were you wearing?

The Last Time You Were In Public Transport - You know the drill by now. Car, Bus, Plane, Taxi, Tuktuk? Was your heart beat fast or slow, were you tense, uncomfortable, why?

The Last Time You Watched A Movie Or Read A Book - Do you have a specific chair, position or room you need to be in? Have you ever fallen asleep while doing this? Does noise make you lose concentration?

The Last Time You Day Dreamed - Where were you? What was it about? How long did it last? Did it keep coming back? Did you fall asleep?

When you are answering the questions and coming up with some more elements that would fit into these different states, be as detailed as you can. This way you can develop a physical awareness of what you are doing when you shift into a state that does not align to the situation that you are in. This way you will be able to make sure that you are performing at the most optimal level that you can when in all scenarios. So what can we begin to do with all this new data in relation to your thoughts and feelings? Let me describe a hypothetical for you if I may. Simply because I don't know what your response to the inventory will be. Let us say that when standing in a queue for the

Bus you noticed that you rocked back and forth between leaning all of your weight onto one leg and then the other. In addition to this you would occasionally hold your breath and let it out whilst puffing your cheeks. Disengaged towards everyone else that is there and simply letting the music on your headphones wash over your unconscious as you wait for your ride.

A similar situation arises when you are talking to someone at work. This someone however holds a position of importance. The rocking on your feet begins, disengagement has begun. If you are to hide this or hold on to the focus needed to discuss whatever this senior person wants to then you would need to curtail this rocking whilst maintaining your physical comfort. By virtue of the fact that you acknowledged the rocking as a link towards disengagement, you become more reactive to it.

From what we learned in the failed Libet experiments we now have the beginnings of a warning system to respond to before the full emotional interference takes control. The alpha state response from the Bus queue does not align with the SMR state requirement for a conversation with a superior. The more comprehensive the inventory is that you develop, the more reactive you can become when possible situations arise that would force a misalignment between brain wave state and response. This way you can be as observant and vigilant as is within your power to be, no matter the scenario you end up in. Akin to the developmental stages Maria Konnikova went through when writing *The Biggest Bluff.*

Quieting the Storyteller

The storyteller is the title that I give to that little voice that lives inside your head. Not in a mental health way but we all have an inner monologue (this is forgetting those who have Aphantasia). This is the direct link to Neuroses, to capabilities, to actions, thoughts, words and is pretty much that thing that is the most capable of influencing what we do. This can also restrict our capability to access memories and act in a way that is required. The arguable route of the antagonistic reasoning if you will.

This is the voice that contributes to the challenge in exercising following the previously stated hypothetical in regards to your feelings when coming home from work. This storyteller works in alignment with your brainwave states and their responses. Working in these different states to develop your control between them may feel a little cerebral and silly at times but the upside of it is complete cognitive control over that little voice in your head. The headphone game that I adapted from the work of Colin Cherry and first put into The Monographs is another fantastic resource here. Elizabeth Loftus leads the field in the area of Memory and the interference of reality. The Misinformation effect shows us some strong imperfections when it comes to memory. Suggestibility can influence others' expectations on our memory and misattribution, information attributed to an incorrect source.

In one such study that played a role in changing the way that witness questioning was to be completed it was revolving around people who had witnessed a car crash of some sort. For those that were questioned about a car crash, they had described dented doors and broken glass on the floor and for those that were questioned about a collision, they had described more noises and speed between the cars. The truth of the matter being that they had both seen the same incident and it was nothing more than a fender bender. To put this into context for us, the witnesses had had a misalignment between wave state and task due to the specific stimuli and the discomfort that provided as they are not used to seeing things of this nature. Therefore their memories are decidedly less accurate. I actively encourage you to dive into Elizabeth Loftus' work and the nature of all memories being false.

We need to be able to memorise, observe and catalogue what we see, hear and smell on a daily basis. As well as during those times that we are afforded the opportunity to focus. All the while 'life' will be going on around us. The storyteller, once controlled, will work to give us a sort of switch for us to turn our awareness off and on after a while. Helping us to climb Noel Burch's ladder of competence in a much more direct way. Creation of awareness through controlling states and our response. You do not have to be the terminator to process everything you see and recognise the red flags, you just have to know what they are. This is why we are here, to get the tools in order to deal with this. During a conversation, were someone to hold up a red flag you wouldn't have to be intently focused to realise its presence and what it means.

Our voice inside our heads tells us what we are capable of and what we are not, tells us if we are going to remember certain things or we are not, tells us if we can recall and deal with certain things or not. We build control over this using time and awareness of our physical changes between states.

Neuroplasticity

What is it? And why, in Dawkins' name, should we care? Neuroplasticity refers to the brain's ability to adapt. Or, as Dr. Campbell puts it:

> "*It refers to the physiological changes in the brain that happen as the result of our interactions with our environment. From the time the brain begins to develop in utero until the day we die, the connections among the cells in our brains reorganise in response to our changing needs. This dynamic process allows us to learn from and adapt to different experiences*" – Celeste Campbell (n.d.).

When we learn something new, we create new connections between our neurons. We rewire our brains to adapt to new circumstances. This happens on a daily basis, but it's also something that we can encourage and stimulate. This type of reorganisation within the brain uses a process referred to as Axonal Sprouting. For us to be able to see something in the world, however vast in size and then catalogue this, process the non-verbal communication details and come to an Inductively reasoned answer within a few seconds and while under pressure is going to take time. We can develop this neuroplastic response through completing drills over and over again until it gets to the point where it just happens automatically.

'You see but you do not observe' is built on the foundation of this. We have a foundation of learning that is based on the idea of monotony. We all know the alphabet and yet it is quite the struggle to say it backwards or name the 18th letter without counting. Yet we can learn to drive and compute, calculate and react to multiple streams of information at the same time as well as having a conversation with a passenger, changing the song on the CD player. We can learn to bring this into our work here in the development of a Sherlockian Memory Palace.

This relates to the learning curve of developing a new skill or attribute. It will take a little time for the neurons to fire together and therefore wire together. We are given these ideas that are drip fed into the way we view our brain and what it is and is not capable of.

We have these moments that we react to by telling ourselves this same story in different versions over and over again. Now I am not saying that you can merely imagine yourself more aware, it takes time and patience like most things. However, when you are feeding yourself negative stories they infect your perception, and in a way they can shape your thinking. So let's take every single moment to change your presence in every scenario, all the time. Tell yourself a better story. The next time you need your keys and the information is not immediately present, try saying I'll get them later as opposed to I can't find them. As Holmes would say, the little things are infinitely the most important. This is something you develop with control over the storyteller and in turn is made easier by virtue of having an awareness of when you shift between brainwave states.

With this way of thinking and change of mindset, your presence in every moment is heightened. You have more retention of each moment because you feel differently about information and therefore become sharper because each stream of information that you see and hear can be dealt with by you. Just as I am sure you have never made notes while watching a movie at the theatre.

 This will take you through to a video example of this Sherlockian Memory development in practice. This is specific to the way that I use the techniques in this book; however, these are just as applicable for parents in the house as they are Lawyers in an office. So what you will have by the end is a series of tools for you to make sure that you are never without any detail that would be a requirement for you to complete your task. There is an endgame in mind that we are working towards here. Once we have developed sufficient control levels over our responses to the information that is presented to us, we are able to tackle any kind of problem or concern that Gregson or Lestrade should bring to us.

The End Game

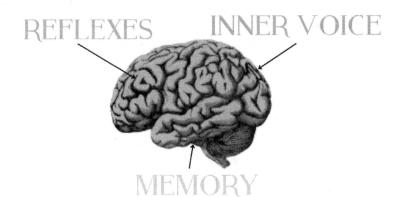

A triangle is not only, geometrically speaking, one of the strongest structures but when it comes to bringing that kind of strength to our mindset, the transient properties are similar. When presented with something and as a matter of reflex we say to ourselves 'I'll never figure that out', your inner voice agrees and starts to remind you of similar occasions where you have struggled to solve a problem, your body starts to follow suit, solidifying the experience and then you are denied access to memories/information that you might need to help. When one element of this is not as strong as it could be, the whole thing starts to fall apart. So with that in mind, I will say it again. Working through these ideas may feel a little cerebral and silly at times. Once you commit to them you will find a resilience to your mindset that you haven't experienced before.

Cultivation and Development

As I tell all people that come to me to learn and develop these skills, the mindset training is something you will do from now on. Our states of mind are not fixed and therefore require consistent maintenance in order to be as sharp as our individual job role requires. So the more we can tap into how best to train these attributes if we are not consistently working is something that we are wise to get to grips with. One cannot hope to develop any longevity with this skill set if the diligence is not there to maintain it. This is another one of those times where cultivation would be easy to explain but it is the completion of the tasks that remain somewhat challenging.

We can understand it a little more directly if you think of it in terms of a basic gym routine. Depending on your split you may be doing legs one day, back and biceps the next and start switching up the cardio and hypertrophy work in between. So you would take the example, physical and emotional responses to specific brainwave states and then push them. Take something that is potentially easy and then make it challenging. If you can deadlift 205 then you shoot for 210. Beta state level activity such as high level exercise and let's say for example that you exhibit huge chest breathing through your mouth as well as leaning forward to place your hands on your knees when you are standing in order to try and catch your breath. What critical thinking game or observation exercise can you play during these moments in order to test yourself? For me during these moments it is something that would require my formal engagement of my amygdala, hippocampal territories, the cerebellum and prefrontal cortex. Either listening to a podcast or taking a class in one of the languages I am learning or at the very least I will be listening to a book. After the beta state activity has been completed, I will test myself. Talk through what the podcast or the book was about, or try and talk in one of the languages I am learning. The specifics of each exercise can be tailored towards you and this is the important point to take away. What puts me into a beta state will not be the same for you and vice versa.

>'Knowing is not enough, we must apply. Willing is not enough, we must do' - Bruce Lee

The type of exercises that you can complete are many and varied. Books can be recited, information catalogued, details memorised and stored. The point is that we can always be growing, learning, refining and developing our banks of knowledge and attributes that will make us more efficient at what we do. It is something that I can only wholeheartedly urge you to do. However this is heavily reliant upon your initiative here. I can only tell you that at the time of writing this, having drilled this daily for a decade, the benefit of this training far outweighs the act itself. My rationality and focus grows with each passing day.

When dealing with the majority of 'problems' (or whatever other word you want to insert in here is fine) the first and primary thing that will hold you back and prevent yourself from solving them is your emotional qualities. Take Einstein for example. When working at the patent office he referred to this as his 'worldly cloister' where he hatched his most beautiful ideas. Freed from any kind of entanglement at the time, his mind can roam free. Take the everyday example of struggling to remember your dreams. You wake up and tell someone that you had the most interesting dream last night. They obviously enquire and you pull up nothing, get frustrated and then it just becomes more difficult to remember. The day goes by and then all of a sudden it is like your brain decides to show you what you needed earlier. The more we build on the control in this area, the more access we have to all of the information needed to do what we do. This is directly relevant when it comes to accuracy of your memory and your ability to focus.

Reasoning 2.0

'It is a capital mistake to theorise before one has data. Insensibly one begins to twist facts to suit theories instead of theories to suit facts'.

This is where the majority of the fun within the world of 'reading people' lies. The number of variables to observations that are made is potentially huge. Should anyone tell you that by simply observing *this* then it would mean *that,* then simply put they are lying to you or very misinformed. Rarely, if ever, will you be presented with an observation you can make that will lead you to an outcome you are certain of. The information is ongoing and subject to potential change as you continue your interactions. One of my colleagues at Procypher - Jim Wenzel, a man who has held more security and military positions of significance than I can remember (which is a lot considering I can remember a great many things), has a rule of three when it comes to the practical assessment of information; Validate, dismiss, clarify. Once you get used to tackling the significance of information being subject to change, you will remain more reactive to these elements.

Here is what we aren't going to do, we aren't going to go over the full details of Deduction, Induction and Abduction. This is because I am going to operate on the basic premise that if you have this version, then you have gone through one of the versions of the first edition of The Monographs. So rather than waste your time we will stick solely to what works and why. The key to the reasoning of information from an observation is knowing what questions to ask yourself based on what you see. The challenge with writing this chapter is to break down a process that is continually in flux. There are a number of elements to consider and rationalise through before you are in a position to decide what is pertinent and what isn't in relation to your deductive goals. Here is a simplistic premise for you to build on:

1. The Outstanding Principle
2. Give it life
3. Questions

These 3 steps alone can be used to gain insight to almost all situations and the best part is, you can use these today. These steps will allow you access to the information that you have in your heads already from simply being alive. The more resources you have in your mnemonic recesses will depend on how engaged in your life you actually are. The fact (a bold statement I know) remains that you very often know a lot more than you give yourself credit for. Take this step for example, have you ever played a card game? A card game of any sort I mean. Specifically one that uses playing cards. Doesn't matter whether it is Magic, Poker or a drinking game. Here is my question for you:

'Can you describe the expression on the King of Clubs' face?'

This may seem like an outlandish and ridiculous question, however I urge you to take this as seriously as you can and to really think about it for as long as you feel you need to in order to come up with an answer. Even if you can only picture the answer in your head. Could you go even further to tell me if he has any facial hair and if he does, what kind? Is he holding anything? Can you answer any of these? Really, really think of it. Please, I know this is just a book but please, please do not cheat. When you have this information, turn to the back of the book to check your work. My point in asking you this is to show you that even with something as random and ridiculously accurate as the expression on the face of a random playing card that you will get an answer of sorts. Your experience of these events involving playing cards has left its informational mark, you only need the right question in order to gain access to it. At what point in time did you ever stop to memorise the faces of the pictures on playing cards? I would argue that you probably didn't, and yet the information is there. So let's take each of the aforementioned steps in turn and break them down.

The Outstanding Principle

This doesn't relate to anything that is good or amazing, simply that which stands out to you. It will be in relation to what stands out to you about whatever it is that you are observing. At its core, that is the most beneficial part of this principle as there is no wrong answer and we are looking to force ourselves past that most difficult of challenges in this moment, starting. There was a gameshow in the early 90's that I used to watch as a kid called 'Catchphrase'. Presented by the most charming Irishman you could ever hope to see, a man by the name of Roy Walker. In this show, contestants would be presented with various images in an 8 bit style, sort of like the NFT's that have become very popular at the moment. These would depict popular catchphrases. If the image was a man holding a bird whilst looking at some shrubberies in the corner where there were 2 more, the contestants would have to buzz in and say, '*A bird in the hand is worth 2 in the bush*'. When anyone would struggle, Roy would encourage them by saying ,"Just say what you see." That really stuck with me as an insight into just getting out of your own way.

The reason this contributes to the strength of our collective mindsets and focuses our abilities in the moment is because there is no wrong answer. You are simply capitalising on an observation to start you thinking. You start from what stands out to you the most. Let's take me again as an example here. You might look at me and see that I am quite stocky or heavily tattooed. What does it take to become big built? Routine, diligence, hard work, goal orientated. This alone can tell you enough about me to begin a read of what I am like as a person. This is a spark for social engineering or information you can use to garner a relationship or control a meeting. You can see just my forearms and my hands (I have many other tattoos however with my forearms and hands, you would stand a good chance of seeing them on a daily basis), this would tell you about my likes, passions, my job not being a conventional one as tattoos are generally frowned upon and this tells you some fields that I may work in. You can then couple that with the fact that I am quite big built and just from a look at my forearms, you can know a laundry list of information that at the same time is very intimate to my life.

The outstanding quality can be haircuts, suit styles, one person standing further away from the others, a particular smell, the car they drive. The point is, if it stands out in society, enough that you notice, then this is information that the situation does not mind telling you. Information that a person is comfortable with you knowing because it means the most to them and they wear it like a badge of pride.

 This code on the left will take you to a video that exemplifies my feelings towards the frustration I have with myself 'in the moment'. All the way to 1 min 30 secs anyway. I will leave its joyous sentiments as a surprise for you. Though it is very poignant. Anyway, back to the method. With an acknowledgement of that which stands out, you can avoid (not remove as we aren't robots) the dissonance of concern we have when reading a person or situation. You often hear the 'Oh god what if I am wrong?' saga. With the application of this principle, you will always and I mean always, have something to work with. If you are in a situation and you find that you don't, then this would mean that you are more concerned with yourself and your views at this time and not how the information you are observing is being communicated to you. Let's build this out then, one step at a time. With the code on the next page you will get a photo. Give yourself 5 seconds and no longer. With this being a book I can only encourage you to test yourself but you will only do yourself a disservice if you take longer. All I want you to do is to make a mental note of that which stands out to you. Which could be anything, ANYTHING.

Ready? 3…2…1…GO!

Take a breather, turn the page and just do your best not to keep thinking about what you noticed. There is a method to the madness, trust me.

Give it life

This is an approach that will be different for those with Aphantasia and it is because of 'that voice' in your head. If you call your internal voice your inner dialogue, self-talk, internal speech, or stream of consciousness, an internal monologue is the voice inside your head that you can "hear" when you think. Initially it was a term coined by Russian psychologist Lev Vygotsky in the early 20th century, he believed that inner speech was a natural part of the thought process[2]. Since then, our understanding of the internal monologue has expanded and changed. As a result of things like Aphantasia and other such marvellous things that the human brain is capable of doing. Have you ever heard about Foreign Accent Syndrome?! Our brains are incredible!

Giving an observation life is a way to practise getting the information away from this potentially harmful little voice. We need to build control over that response so get it out of your head and into a place where it is more tangible and easier to manipulate initially. To give an observation life is to say it out loud or write it down, either way, make your thoughts solid. This way you can proactively take stock of your reads in training as you won't have to look through hindsight, which sadly is 20/20. It is the difference between looking at someone passing you by in the High street and thinking 'He looks like a family man, he doesn't smoke and is going to a jewellers' and saying 'that man is a family man, he does not smoke and is proposing soon.'

If you just think about this information, your reaction time is slower to the clues around you as you don't have to be too aware of said clues in order to come to that conclusion. However when you say it out loud, it exists and you get to take stock of the reasons why you deduce what you do. This gives you a feedback approach in your learning that you don't get from silent cognition. As a point of note, the opposite is true when you are working jobs with these attributes, these ideas are strictly for training. Next time you are around someone you find attractive, just say it out loud instead of thinking it and watch as everything around you becomes more tangible and ultimately the situation fails. This takes care of the fear when confirming your deductions.

What you are doing in announcing this process is taking your thoughts out of your head where your own internal dialogue cannot affect it. Almost everyone has this little voice in their heads that states

29

if they can or cannot do things. This is all that is holding you back here. When you have an idea, you write it down, if you have some jobs to do today, you make a to do list. Once the actions are whole and in front of you, you can analyse them more clearly. The more you do this, the quicker your deductive connections will come. You are building your cognitive reflexes. This is in opposition to Socrates' concern with writing things down and having a good memory but we will cover that when it comes to the memory chapter.

So you have an observation that you have made that is not within reach of your 'storytelling voice' in your head. You can manipulate this from as many different rational directions as you would like now. Not at all like when it was in your head and you have to deal with the demeaning questions that are floating around in there in the early stages. 'Is this relevant?' 'How is this related to what I am looking at?' 'What have I missed?' 'Am I wrong?'. It is in front of you now like an object that you can spin around and look at. I encourage you to now do this with your mental list of outstanding observations that you made from the previous photo. Say them out loud and absolutely do not, I repeat, do not go back and look at the photo again.

Questions

This initially may sound like a way to glaze over more than a century of research into pragmatics and critical thinking but, we can get into this. For now, this is something that will get you thinking about your observations in such a way that takes them past the aesthetic qualities of what you are seeing. One of the games I like to play with my students is something I call *'What is a cup?'*

A game that has simplicity built into its title but can, when the time frame is sufficient enough, be mentally exhausting. Imagine a scene where there is a cup on the table in front of you, wherever this may be in your imagined setting. My question to you as we stand next to each other is:

Me - *What is that?*
You - *It's a cup.*
Me - *Yeah but, what is that?*
You - *It is something someone would drink from.*
Me - *What else?*

We would keep going in this way for around 20 minutes in the early stages. In this way you can start to make yourself aware of the variables within a situation. Now it sounds like a hell of a cognitive load to bear and in the early stages of practice it absolutely is. However, when you are aware of more of these you will be able to be more accurate in your reads by virtue of the fact that you are aware of more implications. Once you start to add in the personal insights that you can see then these variables will mean things like a cup is no longer just a cup it will be things like 'this is the subject's favourite cup. As a night shift worker there is a coffee addiction of sorts. The subject needs more water in their diet and will likely have lower back mobility/pain issues as a result. Registering as Autistic, likely someone with Aspergers though I would need more information to

31

confirm. Right handed and around 5'8" tall'. That's a true story from a remote assessment I was hired to give. It all started with a cup which then led to variables and then confirmation with other aspects within the room.

This is something that will be a challenge to many at the start as it is a little like being thrown into an Improv comedy group. Something that I actually believe the cast of Whose Line Is It Anyway would be very good at. If you are familiar with this show then the props game is a joy to behold. Let's take it out for a walk so to speak. You will need to get some paper and a pen. Seriously, get some. Either that or open the notes app on your phone. Here is a photo:

Now all you have to do is to answer the question *'What is this?'* 10 times as fast as you can. Here are some things that you should note about 'as fast as you can'. If you can answer the question 10 times in 2 minutes, then the time is fast but if you can answer the question 10 times in 30 minutes then the responses are slow and thought out.

Avoid cheating by using slang and synonyms. The question is referring only to the cup and not me holding it. Really think about this. You will of course probably breeze past this but I urge you to play along.

How did you find that? Horrible? Awesome. This is something to build upon. I will include my suggestions here as well for how I would have answered that.

1. A coffee cup
2. A rather big cup
3. A cup that would likely be used by a big person
4. A cup that is used by a very thirsty/greedy person
5. An indicator of eccentricity
6. An indicator of someone young at heart
7. A cup that has been recently used
8. Something someone could use to keep warm in the right scenario
9. Something that could also be used for soup
10. An indicator of someone who is a fan of The Muppets.

What you have here is an initial understanding of the first level of information that you can consider. A cup will never be just a cup anymore. Freeing up your prefrontal cortex to process more and more. To continue the game we simply add more and more context. So, the same question, answered the same number of times but you consider the whole photo now. The question remains the same, what is the cup? Go!

What you should have now is a consideration for the first stage of information in relation to a grander contextual insight. So as food for thought I offer you my 10 again:

1. Indication of someone spending a lot of time at the table
2. Someone who is likely right handed, given there a computers there
3. A big coffee drinker
4. Indicator of someone who struggles with sleep
5. Indicator of someone with a sweet tooth
6. Indicator of someone who likely has a large hand
7. A companion for someone who spends a lot of time working on a computer
8. Indication of someone for whom cleanliness is not a priority
9. Indication of a recent commencement of work

10. Indication of recently returning from a break

With this approach you build your possible understanding of something by virtue of the distance between you and it. I adapted this from the way a Therapist friend of mine described how people with Depression feel about themselves at times. If you imagine looking at a glass on a table, you might see the clear liquid inside and see that it is a red glass. You get closer and see a little chip on the lip as well as thumbprints from previous use. A little closer and you can smell that it is vodka and not water. You will keep getting closer and closer until you get to the stage where you will see that the molecules of the glass are not even touching. This highlights the struggle for mental health that many people face but what I took from this is that there is a degree of enhancement to the observations that we make. A perceptual circumstance if you will. Information can have more potential to change when we change our relationship to it. Be it by distance or by angle or both. This is something I would urge you to never forget when moving forward in your training. It will help to keep you in a continual zone of confirmation. We are dealing with non-verbal communication (think of that more as a blanket term, applying to information that simply is not said) and this is not finite at all. It is constantly in flux as all humans are. Your information will follow suit in accordance with this. The degree to which it changes will depend on the context you are viewing it in i.e. whether viewing it remotely for an assessment or live and in person in some way.

Going back to the photo of 6 men in a bath...or was it 7, can you remember? Did you just tell me the number or did you have a brief moment where you second guessed yourself? There is your first feedback from training within reasoning, your engagement in information. If you second guess yourself however briefly then what that means is that you had a moment where your brainwave state was not aligned with the situation. Maybe triggered by a momentary fear response or nervousness but whatever it was you can now learn from it. You take that felt state detail and fold it into your developing behavioural inventory. In addition, you know that for you, the stand out observation was not the number of people that were there, that was likely secondary to the details you were noticing in each person. Whereas if you unquestioningly knew what the answer was then you have the converse information to fold into your training. You have a felt state response to control, and the number of certain things is something that you engage with more readily than say the design on a t-shirt for example. It is information like this that you can then use to push your training further as you will learn more and more about what your comfort levels are and how to change them.

This is what I would refer to as a developmental practice of reasoning. The reason being is that it will be something that will never end in the pursuit of competency. You may be thinking something along the lines of "*OK so I can look at something and figure out what it means. How is that anything to do with reasoning? What about Deduction?*" That Bloody buzz word! I kid but it still amazes me that there seems to be a confusion about the names of certain things and implying that there is some other 'method' or 'trick' to it all. Of course you may not have been thinking that but based on the emails I get there are a few. So here it is, reasoning is built into the above practice.

Whether this be through Deduction, Induction or Abduction these are all processes of reasoning. The logical process of obtaining information from something by exploration of the variables it suggests in order to arrive at the most likely outcome. The three terms are in relation to the direction of the questions you are asking yourself about what it is that you have seen. Deduction would go forwards in time from what you have seen. For example, if I know someone has had a lot to drink, I can deduce that they will need to go to the bathroom soon after and if they don't, then comparing the 'volume' of liquid to the rate of consumption I can deduce that there is some kind of issue. Abduction would be going backwards from what it is that you have seen to get to some details. For example, if I walk into a kitchen and see an empty birthday cake box, as well as 2 remaining slices on the tin foil wrapped cardboard that usually comes with it then I can abduce that there has been some sort of Birthday celebration. However minute this may be. Induction, the method more in line with the strictest Holmesian practice would be to do with likelihoods.

Take the same abductive example I gave but the cake box is just a run of the mill store bought cake and there are no obvious candles lying around. We can abduce some kind of a birthday party but we can combine abductive and inductive reasoning to infer that very likely there has been some sort of celebration. When dealing with English culture this is very likely a Birthday but it can also be for new jobs/positions, Christmas, housewarming and a slew of others. This raises something else in the practice of reasoning in that the questions you ask yourself can be specific to the information you need from a situation. What does that mean? Design yourself a purpose!

Have a purpose

I like to think I am something of an eloquent kind of guy and yet, to me, there are few who have described the power of purpose within the context of Reasoning better than Agent Smith from The Matrix Trilogy. Here it is:

'There's no escaping reason, no denying purpose, for as we both know, without purpose we would not exist. It is purpose that created us, purpose that connects us, purpose that pulls us, that guides us, that drives us; it is purpose that defines us, purpose that binds us.'

We can use this as a way to direct the reasoning of information in use when we are working. Doing our best to make the cognitive load that we have to bear a little lighter. Take the photo from before with all of us in the paddling pool. When I said to you before, make a note of what stands out, this will be enough to get you started on the way to obtain information from that which you observe. Now when I tell you, your purpose in looking at the photo is to give me an answer to this question *'Why was the photo taken?'*. Now, what you can do, even before you look at the photo, is to think 'Why are photos taken?' Commemoration, celebration, commiseration, remembrance, social media gloating? Then give yourself 5 seconds and now look at the photo. Make a note of everything that stands out to you. This time when you explore those things that were found when using the outstanding principle you get to have a clarity on whether or not it is pertinent to your goal. It is only after you have fully explored something that you noticed that you would be able to comment on whether or not it is going to help you on your quest. You can apply the same creation of purpose to your training. Yes you are going to train but what? And to what end?

Are you going to memorise a deck just for the sake of memorising a deck or are you going to do it because you want the challenge of being able to do it through your periphery? Are you going to practise your reasoning for the sake of saying 'I trained Reasoning today' or are you going to practise reasoning specific information using only photos? How are you going to confirm? This is the flaw in the 10,000 hours rule that seems to elude a great many people. If any of the 10,000 hours you spend aren't specific or lack direction then mastery is something that you won't achieve. It becomes about the development of a routine and taking advantage of those moments that are presented to you as part of your day where you can get some training in for free, at no detriment to anything else you might be doing. Spending 10,000 hours doing something will not get you competency at something by being passive to its wisdom. You need to engage! As much as each specific moment will allow, as that degree will change.

The more you channel this into your work, the more you will notice each opportunity that is presented to you as a chance to sharpen your reasoning skills. Be warned though, it can bleed over into all facets of your life. Take for example something as workaday as time in the break room where you work. I have frequented many offices throughout my life and probably will frequent quite a few more, at least I hope so anyway! When in the break room I would try and reason what people were eating or drinking based on what i could smell, or who was entering the door behind me by the sounds of the shoes and who I could remember was wearing what kind of shoes. These daily drills all added up to something that after a few months of continual work, became second nature. This allowed me to focus my attention on other things I may have been working on at the time. Trust me when I say that your ability to reason and your mindset should be the aspects that are at the top of your continual training regimen. I run a 10 week course on reasoning alone! To me, this is how important it is. Without your ability to reason, the information you notice will remain as quirky anecdotes than anything else.

The Emotional Qualities

I am sure that the people who train with me get sick to death of hearing me harp on about them and yet, emotional qualities are something that we all fall foul of. All of us. Think about it within the context of insults. Whatever the words that are used are, they are designed to stop people from thinking clearly in the moment and affect some sort of change. I will give you an example from my youth.

I have always had a big head (I mean my cranium despite what those in the comment section may say). When I was 3 years old, I was the pageboy for a friend of the family's wedding. I had to wear a suit for the occasion and of course, a top hat. Only for a 3 year old, I had to wear an XL Men's size hat! This has not changed, the growth of my body has changed around this.

The photos are included for your amusement. During primary school and early high school I was bullied something fierce because of the size of my head. They would call me names and draw comparisons to things like the 'Hey Arnold' cartoon. In the opening credits one of the other characters would shout at Arnold ,"Move it football head!' I remember one particular incident in the Rainbow garden, one of the young lads Simon was trying to get a rise out of me.

Simon: *Look at the size of it, you look like a fucking mutant!*
Me: *I know right, its massive*
Simon: *Yeah, I would hate that*
Me: *It'll be alright, it will all level out in the end*

I remember just being confused by him making statements of fact that were designed to be insulting. I do have a big head. No matter the tone of voice he used, that was an irrefutable truth. Now imagine if I actually felt bad about my head or self-conscious in some way. There would be quite the change between the 2 examples. Crying and even more emotional damage would have likely ensued. I continued this kind of philosophy towards emotional control, even long before I started on this journey. It was a key element in a lot of the martial arts gyms I went to.

'I am gonna smash your face in Ben!!'
'Actually Dave you aren't, that's murder and we are sparring. Think it through please'

.....True story.

My point is not that I am clearly on the spectrum in some way but more that because I thought about the words being said just a little bit longer, that I had no 'emotive response' to the desired action and I was able to respond to the situation as best my skill set would allow. Insults only exist because they are something we feel bad about, the person has some sort of perceived authority over us or both. I saw this again in the most glorious of action movies, Roadhouse. Patrick

Swayze is telling the staff that if someone shouts at you, be nice. If they swear at you, be nice. You can be nice until it is time not to be nice. Then one of the other guys yells out *'Yeah but what if he calls my mother a whore?'* to which Mr. Swayze elegantly responds, *'Is she?'* Beautifully illustrated right?!

The degree to which an emotive reaction can shift the perception of the situation for you is down to your emotional intelligence. This will give a wider understanding of handling the situation. So for those who already have a strong degree of Emotional intelligence you can skip on a few pages. For the rest of us, there has been a lot of work in this area and testing where the arrows point to one side and then the other. I will do my best to sum it up as succinctly as I can. Your emotions can influence an evaluative judgement of a situation that is seen through whatever mood you are in. If you are sad for example, you might not find something funny that you usually would. Speaking strictly of neuroscience, we know that there can't be a complete removal of our biases. However we can learn to diminish their responses and control their influence. It is a call back to the techniques we spoke of in the first chapter, it is just that we can't not reference this when discussing reasoning as the 2 methods are intrinsically linked.

Examples

On the podcast we like to have a moment of testing riddles in this way. They are small stories that are designed to affect your emotional state because they become a struggle to resolve when you can't rationally put the pieces together. In other words, when you have an emotive response. Watching a good magic trick can have the same effect. On one of these many occasions Adam set the scene by asking me to solve a riddle that had kept him going for days and was really annoying him at this stage. It went like this:

'You are in a sealed room with no air. All the windows are locked and the keys are dangling on a hook outside that you can see. Maybe a few feet away from you. You have a table, a chair and some food. The room starts to fill with water. How do you escape?'

Now you can take some time over this if you would like but just know that the answer is coming now so do whatever you need to, to make sure that you don't see it if you want to play. After he had laid down the gauntlet, quite proudly might I add, my response was only a second or 2 after but I said ,"Use the door?" His jaw dropped and then several expletives were used that I shouldn't type here. The drama of the setting was designed to make you think immediately about action in the room. Sealed, and locked windows were designed to imply everything was locked. My first thought after he told me the riddle was, just because you didn't say anything about the door doesn't mean there isn't one. You can take the same approach to riddles as you can to the use of the 3 step method when using real world situations. Here is another one for you:

'A Japanese boat was stuck in water because of the storm, and after the storm, the captain was found dead. The engineer was busy fixing the signals, the cook was managing the wine barrels, the wife went to

the room, and the maid was fixing the upside-down turned flag. Who killed the captain?'

You may already have some idea or possibly have even heard it before. However please go with me while I Illustrate the application of the method using this approach. When you look at that riddle, what are the elements that would present themselves when using the outstanding principle? I present mine here for you:

- Japanese boat
- The storm
- The captain's death
- The engineer and the signals
- The cook and the wine barrels
- The wife going to her room
- The maid with the flag

We can then give each of the elements life and ask ourselves questions in order to explain each of them using our purpose. The purpose being to find out who killed the captain. Let's check them off one at a time.

- Japanese boat - Relates to the need for a flag maybe? The Japanese flag has a white background with a red circle in the middle
- The storm - Never mentioned as being anything that relates to a cause of death and is illustrated as a distraction for the killer to work. We can forget about this for now.

45

- The Captain's death - The captain died during the storm. When on a boat in a storm, all of the crew have specific tasks to carry out to make sure everyone stays safe. The killer will be the one who is doing something they shouldn't be, maybe.
- The engineer and the signals - I googled an engineer's job when at sea. Fixing signals relates to the internal stats and dials that are used. This could be something that the engineer was actually doing.
- The cook and the wine barrels - Cooking wine maybe? Either way this is something that the cook could very well be doing.
- The wife going to her room - Whose wife is this? Probably the captains. Why was she going to her room? An argument? An escape? She may not have a role on the ship and be there just because she is someone's wife. She could very well just be going back to her room. We could ask further questions regarding the motivation to do so though.
- The maid with the flag - Folding and tidying is part of a maid's duties. How do you have an upside down flag though? Even more so with the Japanese flag.

…The maid did it.

This is how we can start to apply these methods and practices towards all manner of observations and the more we use them, even on the seemingly insignificant elements of our day, the more accuracy and speed becomes inherent in the process. Once more then, by yourself this time and I challenge you to follow the process but not to make any notes.

'The prisoner was locked up in a room with a dirt floor. The room has one window, which is high up above the prisoner's height. The prisoner had a shovel, but he had only 2 days to get out, and digging would take him more than 5. How would he escape?'
The answer will be at the back of the book.

In conclusion you could spend many hours researching and concerning yourself with the specific details of what exactly Deductive, Inductive and Abductive reasoning is and how the terminology should be defined in relation to its use. If you choose to do that then as far as application goes, this is a lot of wasted time. You can call the process whatever you want for all I care. Application and use of the material itself is all that matters to us here. So moving forward with this would depend entirely on what you want the knowledge for. If it's speculative, research of some sort or you had a few bucks you didn't mind trying your luck with then by all means, continue with the data mining. However if it is that you are looking for these methods to be able to gain you actionable information from people then please take heed of all of the prompts given in order to have these skills ready to use at a moment's notice. The purpose being to gain yourself some heuristics to be able to look towards when the situation has a requirement for them.

Moulding more clay into bricks

L'homme c'est rien - l'oeuvre c'est tout (The man is nothing, the work is everything)

What is life without our memories? I am not getting contemplative and thought provoking all of a sudden, it is a serious question. What is life without our memories? The answer is a simple but dark one, at least for me anyway. We wouldn't be anywhere. We wouldn't be anything. Think about everything you decided to do and the opinions you have developed on topics that form the basis of your interactions with people for example. If you forgot all of these experiences, what would you be? You wouldn't be anything. This is how important our memories are in general. Now when it comes to our work they become even more important. We deal with observations and information that passes by us very quickly at times. How can we even hope to utilise this information if we can't store it and recall it later. Think of the humble benefit for recalling licence plates (we will get to this soon).

In terms of the content for this, the relevant studies and research material will be in the back of the book. For the chapter itself we are going to focus on what works and why. Here will be your first clue as to why mindset and reasoning has been laid out first. These both form foundational parts of how your memory is going to become sharper. When you look at the work of Dr Elizabeth Loftus and the fallibility of our memories it is (if you will allow me to use a gigantic nutshell) emotion that causes the details to crumble around you. This is why we look to build these steps first so that when you see something, regardless of how quickly it moves in front of you, there will be no little voice inside your head that says words to the effect of 'Yeah but, are you sure?'

As we covered links, pegs and the basics of memory palace work the first time, it is only fair that we build on this information a second time. There is something that sits at the base of memory techniques. Something that we should understand how to utilise before we even start to think about reliance on any kind of technique or method no matter how many thousands of years old it is. This is quite simply, engagement. Our capacity for retention is deeply improved by simply engaging with information fully and completely. I realise that I just said simply but as this relies on emotional control, this is not as simple as the word may hope to convey.

Getting engaged to yourself

When you watch a film or binge watch a tv show on Netflix, how many hours of prep or training do you go through in order to do that? I know, that's a stupid question right. You just sit down and watch what you want to. Whenever it is done you have approximately 2 hours' worth of information that you talk to other people who have seen the film about. Characters names, the actors who played them, what you have seen them in before, what they were wearing, where they were going, what they did etc. That is a lot of information right. So why is it that we struggle to do this with the details in a lot of other areas? We engage with films easier than reading last quarter's figures for example. They are there to entertain us, the figures, sadly are not. We can do this by utilising the control over ourselves that we developed in the previous chapters. Purpose and control.

 The QR code at the side here will take you to a random memory test I found on YouTube. You can use this to get an understanding of how it feels to engage in the details. The information in this video is going to go by you very fast. Set your purpose in terms of complete and total engagement in the exercise. There is no 'winning' or 'losing', there is only engaging with the information. The exercise itself is set around a specific memory practice and technique, however the speed will be the charm. If you already know any techniques then specifically do not use them. Simply engage with the information that is shown to you and learn to develop your naturally retentive capacity. Although I know some of you will keep score. What I would like you to take stock of is how it felt physically for you to do this. Factor this into your behavioural inventory as you develop it more and more.

I would encourage you to factor this into your memory training moving forward. Alongside the techniques and everything else as well but what you will get from this is a default level of attention that 90% of people (not an exact number, it's based on interactions with humans) don't seem to have. It relates to the reason why most people seem to think they struggle with remembering names. A lot of the time, if you are one of these people labouring under this misapprehension, it will be the simple fact that you just don't care about the name. If you make that an important part of the conversation you are having with the individual, whether internally or externally, it is up to you, then this will increase your retention. In most conversations where remembering names is important, there are other factors that get in the way. Namely the verbal content of the discussion and internal stress or concern over the importance of the interaction. In addition to this, you can learn to tell yourself better stories.

There has been lots written about the topic of self-talk and the related mental health side effects. Lots of it is ethereal but the important factor to take note of is that this is a link to the founding emotional connection to your beliefs and your capabilities. It is the after effects of your inner monologue. Think about it like this, your inner monologue is the voice and opinions that you hear more than anything else, let alone anyone else. If you are constantly telling yourself that you can't remember names, or you can't deduce or this is really hard or whatever, then you are only making the odds of your success terrible by default. You will eventually learn that you have a terrible memory or whatever other fact you are apparently telling yourself. It's a simple as if you say something like:

> *'I will never remember that'*

Then you need only change it to:

> *'It will come back to me later'*

When you have tried to tell someone about the dream you had that night because it was awesome and weird and involved you playing pool with the animated Hercules only it wasn't with pool balls, they were multicoloured air hockey pucks (actual dream I had) only you struggle with the initial details. In those moments do you say you can't remember? Or do you say I can't remember it at the moment? Those little details and minor changes is something that you can do in order to change the fundamentals of how you think about yourself. When it comes to developing cerebral skills, this is super important!

So the next time you are struggling to recall something or even struggling to memorise something ask yourself how engaged you are or have been with the specifics you need. Do you know why you are doing what you are doing, do you agree with the purpose? Do you want a memory palace of Sherlockian magnitude because you think it's cool as you are a fan or do you have a utilitarian use for one? These are the very important but often overlooked aspects of memory work, particularly when it comes to observational practices. The fascination with a magical method that does most of the heavy lifting for you is something that has to go. I realise that, as I write this, I am starting to sound like an old man on some kind of rant about how the children of today are using apps to do everything for them and I suppose on the one hand I am, but on the other it doesn't make me any less right. You can't learn a few techniques and hope that will do everything for you because you are the person that will have to apply them.

With that being said, let's look at a few methods and techniques that you can use that will take some getting used to. They are a little like the lovechild of link systems and pegging and Cicero and everything else. Everything from the Ancient aboriginal to the developmental parts of synaesthesia. I should point out that I will fully explore any method to see what works for me and the people I teach. Does that mean that every method works or every method does not? No. What this means is that I have specifically made use of these methods over a number of years that are geared specifically to the work I do and many others within this field do as well. They should each have their own use however, until this day I am still no good with Simon Reinhard's number system! I am not frustrated....honest.

Linking for profiling

So it should be of no secret that I am a massive nerd. There, I said it. They say admitting it is the first step towards recovery right? I have heard over the years of teaching this that many people feel like Shawn Spencer when they use it. I don't believe for a second that nobody else has tried this but it is the continual use of this that really lets the details of the technique sink in. Much like the reasoning chapter I am not going to go into the details of the method again as that was covered in the first edition.

With the following picture, allow me to first paint an image for you. You are investigating a business of some sort and its employee's. You need as much personal insight into each of them in order to fulfil the promises that were made during you being hired. You are walking through the office. You notice this on the nearest table as you walk by.

What do you see when you look at this? That's not a philosophical 'cool runnings' type of question where you need to shout at yourself in the mirror for a moment until you have some life altering realisation. Literally, what do you see when you look at this photo? As in if you looked at it and then looked away. 5 minutes later some handsome, bearded fellow says to you 'what was in the picture?'. I realise that in over explaining the point here that many of you will have tacked on additional details or changed the answer in some way and that's fine but if your answer was, at the start, 2 Rubik's cubes then that is a great start but as you create the links for these in your head, the Rubik's cubes you use better not be the conventional ones. This would be remembering a lie. Even if you don't know precisely what kind of Rubik's cubes they are, there is still much more detail to them than a cube. For example:

- One looks like it uses cogs
- One is all silver and funny shapes

- One is solved and the other is not
- One has green and yellow sides so we might infer that this has the other 6 colours too

This alone will create a very strong link that you can use as they already are unconventional items for an everyday occurrence. Link them to the person or location and you are good to go. All standard stuff right? Kind of anyway. Now, make sure you can't see the photo when you look at this next question. Not a question actually, more of a request. Tell me everything you can about the background, and everything else that was not the cubes themselves. Realistically you gave you quite a bit of detail as it was only one photo and there wasn't that much to see. However my point is that when you think of something that exists, you rarely if ever, think of it by itself, there are links to it in your head. Use these! Use these as much and as often as you can. The outstanding principle will get you the core piece of data, as in the cubes, but your engagement in the information will get you additional detail that surrounds it.

Think of your favourite restaurant. Take a moment to picture it. Now whether you are outside of it or inside of it in your head (most of you will be inside the restaurant), you will not just be thinking of the meal or the sign. You will be thinking about everything from when you were last there. Sights, sounds, smells, conversation, ambience, the weather, daytime, night-time, everything. That one time you thought about your favourite restaurant, everything else comes along with it for free. What does this mean for those in observational work? Well, simply put you can now use the link method to rebuild environments and intricate details of specific locations in your head. This is information that you can use in your job role but you can also use this to create new journeys and keep them with you at all times. Like the safari journey I took once 20 years ago in Kenya, or how to get around Paris without a map even if you don't speak the language. The initial link is all you would need as a method of 'storage' because strictly speaking, it isn't stored anywhere. If for some reason during this hypothetical case you are working on; a few weeks later you see someone has dropped their 'Cubing' membership card in a very important location then, if you had gone over the linked information a few times after you saw it initially then you would be given the cube

 connection back by virtue of this link. The tartan, bed and wardrobe in the background would all come along for the ride for free.

Let's put this to the test then! Your direction is very simple, watch the clip and pay attention. Nothing more, nothing less. Use the link method to take stock of everything that stands out for you. It is worth mentioning that this is a 360 degree video so if you have a set of VR goggles then I encourage you to use them so you can really immerse yourself in the practice. Just remember what you see.

I am now assuming that you have done this and have, in adherence with your development, watched the video only once. Next thing to do is to go and do something else for a bit. I am serious. Put the book down and go and take 15 minutes to do something else. I am still deadly serious.

Really. Put it down and go and do something else for a bit.

Good. Now that that's done or you have just humoured me and continued on anyway, here is the proof of the pudding. There is no way for me to know exactly what stood out to you, so I am going to add an array of questions so you can get the feeling for the connections the links made during your mnemonic excursion.

1. Tell me about the guy that spoke about 'being viewed in 360 degrees. What was his complaint? What did he look like? What was he wearing?
2. When we crossed the first road, what direction were we instructed to look?
3. What candy was displayed prominently on the left as we passed? What colour were they?
4. How many street artists did we pass?
5. How many people were in my group?
6. What kind of cinema did we pass?
7. What was the name of the casino?
8. Tell me about the girl with green trousers?
9. What fast food joints were there?
10. What was the name of the film that had been turned into a musical?

I hope you got all of them but even if you got one of them it was to simply illustrate that there is an abundance of information that comes along with a link when used with 'real life' objects and details. Once this has been completed I would encourage building a reflex that drives towards the consolidation of the information. Go over the developed links once, a few minutes after the fact and then again around an hour later just to really seal the information in. This then becomes part of your daily work and is something that you can and should do everywhere you go. From a security perspective you are building into yourselves a base level of heightened awareness of your environment. This is by virtue of the mere employment of a humble memory technique and being present in the moments you are interacting with the situation and others.

The method itself is about driving your attention towards the environment and making the information that you could use that much easier to be able to bring along with you. Mentathlete's and those who go to memory competitions are capable of memorising thousands of digits and pictures, as well as decks and decks of playing cards. The only thing for us is that we have to tune our memories to information of that nature and maybe even that volume, in the real world. We cannot wear sound cancelling headphones or wear blinkers. As such we need to make sure our focus is not taxed, our emotions not challenged and our minds sharp in order to take in and use what we need.

Plates and Pegs

I will preface this by saying pegs is just the easiest and most accessible term that I use for a system that converts less tangible data into something more memorable. There are many, and I mean many to choose from. PAO, Dominic system, Peg system and even something that I published in Sherlock's Memory secrets. The method that is for you is something that you would need to explore. My personal recommendation to start with would be a PAO or Dominic system that will help you turn every number from zero to 99 into people. Especially for the speedy and organic conversions you will have to make, having mnemonic people ready to use is so much easier. The key is to be able to treat the data you see as something that you would be able to read. The QR code here is for the first 100 I use. This should get you started.

 These will no doubt require some drilling to be able to make them your own. Either that or spend some time to be able to create your own. Snap recognition is what you are looking for with this. Once you spend enough time around these images and thoughts then the numbers after a while will not be empty pieces of data, they will provide an immediate prompt to the people you connected them to. This is a necessary evil whether you are in competitions, observational work or both but once it has been done you will likely not have to do something like this again. The system is not the focus of this part of the chapter. It is being able to read the numbers, facts and figures as people and stories and what you do with them once they have been created.

If you were involved in sleight of hand magic the term would be jazzing but in short you won't know precisely which technique you will need when you are in the trenches which is why you will need to be comfortable with these conversions as well as word substitutions and journeys. I will come to the memory palace buzz word shortly as it is nothing like how it is depicted in the media. At least for how I use it anyway. In addition to this we should begin to be more comfortable with Journeys and word substitutions. This will help with the immediacy of 'filing' the information that you can consolidate at a later point. These have been covered in the earlier edition however, just for the sake of completeness, here is a whistlestop tour.

Journeys would be what most folks would refer to as a memory palace but if you know anything about me then you should know I don't really care for terminology, so long as you know what to use and when. This is more important. Journeys are an imagined walk around a location that you know well with pre-determined and specific points. To take a journey in your head. This can be anything from your morning routine of getting out of bed, to the drive to work or even the route around your uncle's house who lives in Australia that you haven't seen for years. As long as it is clear in your head and has a sequence, you can use it. The number of stops and variation of journeys would be your decision but to be clear if you are using your sofa as a stop on the journey and you are trying to save space by having it as 3 points due to it being able to fit 3 people then this will be a direct route to you being confused during your recall. Each space needs to be clear and unencumbered by other points on the journey.

Word substitutions could be considered a simple act of creativity that would get easier with time. The easiest example would be when learning words from a foreign language. I am learning Spanish at the moment and the first word in my Anki deck for today is 'Acabar' this is a verb which means 'to finish'. With word substitutions this could be changed to someone with a cold saying 'A Bar' but it would sound weird due to them having a cold and they are trying to finish their shift in a bar. This could also be a Magician struggling to say Abracadabra so he can finish his trick. The 'trick' to this (no pun intended) is to be able to do this quickly and confidently. Let us not forget that we are dealing with information being thrown at you in the real world so the speed could be the slowest thing you will ever hear but it can also pass by you in the blink of an eye. These elements that you cannot control can possibly influence your capability to retain the details. This will need practice.

Licence Plates

This is the easiest and most convenient method of practice that we can all use to get better at the use of these methods. It is congenial to everyone (pretty much) on the planet. The only thing you will need is access to your smartphone or some other kind of recording device. This is so you can check your work later. What is a test without a review and feedback right?

Set your purpose. Are you just retaining all of the information? Do you want to make sure the information is specific to the cars? Do you want to make sure all of the above is taken care of as well as where you saw the cars as well? The filing of the information is something that will need to be idiosyncratic to your own comfort preferences. Here are some suggestions of basic applications than you can use:

- Retaining all of the information - Use the numbers and substitutions as one giant link system
- Specific to the cars - Separate journeys for separate cars and/or add in an additional image for the car brand to the giant link
- All of the above with the locations - Separate journeys that start with images for the locations.

However please consider those just examples that can be used. You would be better served by exploring methods and testing them out to see which one is right for you. Idiosyncrasies are a requirement in memory work. That is definitely more of an opinion I have on memory work than a fact, though there is a slew of research to back this up.

If I say to you 'Albert Einstein'. What are your first thoughts when picturing this? Is it the patent office? $E=mc^2$? Or just the outlandish hair? Whichever it was, there will have been something that occurred to you first. This would mean that the next time Einstein is mentioned your first prompt will likely be the same thing. Make use of this fact when memorising or observing information. It is like getting a freebie of sorts. You don't want to be stuck in the situation of thinking 'Oh ****
what did Ben say it was again?' as the connection to your own thoughts is not as strong. If we both think of the same thing then

that's fine but I would be willing to bet that we would be thinking about the details around it in very different ways. Idiosyncrasies are something that you should learn to lean into. 31 could attach to many systems in many different ways and yet it will always remind me of the Griffin family from Family Guy. This is because they live at 31 Spooner Street. The Simpsons live at 742 Evergreen Terrace and so that number is only ever connected to The Simpsons for me. I don't think we need to state the number of connotations that 221 can give me either. You are looking to make the memory work accessible and as easy as possible given the volume of detail that could potentially be thrown your way. Instead of vehemently attaching yourself to any system, if there is something else that presents itself more readily then I urge you not to knock this in anyway. This will make your memorised plate much easier to recollect.

Leaning into these elements though will be something that will take a great deal of practice as you will have to battle that inner voice that lives inside of your head. There will be an operatic chorus to words to the effect of 'Is this the right way of doing this?' It will take some time to get used to however it is something that I can only urge that you persist with as not only will your memorised plate become easier to recollect, it will also mean that you gain more control over yourself and confidence in the observations you make.

Now is the time. We must put this to the test. I will give you the first 2 examples to walk you through the process needed to gain all of this information in the most expedient manner. Your purpose as this goes on will be to take as much information in as you possibly can and to be able to recite at least 70% of this even when you have finished the book altogether.

Leaning into the idiosyncrasies, for me the first 2 letters remind me of Pez as in the candy with the fun dispensers. 65 gives me Shannon Elizabeth from my list and PWO reminded me of POW's but I would have to make the last part of whatever they were doing, backwards. I would imagine the Peugeot Lion dispensing Pez to Shannon Elizabeth. Dressed as she is from her infamous scene in American Pie this means she will be a prisoner of war and as she's dragged in, she screams ,"You got the last part backwards!!"

A quick image that would tick all of the available boxes. Now if it is that this car were to speed past me in reality. I might only have the opportunity for this quick little scenario. Should this need to be stored for longevity I can attach this to a journey and then keep going.

So here we go. I can only encourage you to play along as sincerely as possible. Whether you actually do or not will be down to how committed you are to developing these skills for yourself and whereas there is no 'right answer for the skills you are developing this should be a statement that will help you to commit in a way that is best to suited to the environment you are in when you are reading this particular page. There will be some licence plates to follow. You don't know the questions I am going to ask you after the fact so you will need to remember all that you can. Good luck! Do your best to add some additional pressure by turning through the pages as quickly as you dare.

There it is. At this stage don't keep going over and over the information just 'to make sure you have it' because, in line with Socrates' view on writing things down you are imbuing yourself with the nature of forgetting. Learn to build that trust within yourself and it will flow into the strength of your mindset when working. To stand there and state to yourself '*I need to go over this as much as possible so that I don't forget it*' is a very different neuroplastic statement and response to '*I will go over this now, once, to begin consolidation*'.

The challenge at this stage will be learning the creative flex needed to create the images as you see them pass by you. That moment of wondering whether or not it was the right choice is something that I am telling you now, will plague you in the initial stages. So take it slowly and build your tolerance and state control with this measure. Lean into your idiosyncrasies and create with as many of your senses as possible and apply logical order. Simple! Yet practice will be needed as, if you don't have much experience with immediate creation of images the awkwardness will be something you will have to develop control over when you are contesting with the 'speed' of real life.

Any way you want it, that's the way you 'file' it

First of all, yes that was a journey pun and I thank you for going along with me in this. For what we have here, this is a discussion of the many organic uses I have found for the journey method of memorisation. Now, there are some that may misconstrue this as some vain claim to originality, it isn't. My personal belief is that I can't know everything on a topic because I haven't read everything. What this is, is a discussion of my personal findings, my journey if you will (I'm sorry, I'll stop now) of experience with the journey method.

Much like the previous discussion of memory methods in this book, I am writing under the assumption that you have either read the first iteration of The Monographs or you already have some understanding of the techniques at play. So journey methods can be used to store lists of data and be manipulated to such a degree that the order can be reviewed and revised if needed. It can be throughout the course of a day that if you have to deal with a lot of information that you would need to recite in order and with clarity, that the likelihood of you having a single journey with a few hundred steps, is very small. Even if you did, how would you then create the various stoppers along the way to separate the information that you need? Not that that can't be done, it is just that there are easier and more direct ways to accomplish this.

Let's take the doomsday algorithm as an example. I am not tipping the method to this but in case you don't know what it is; it is a way for you to be able to figure out the day of the week for any date given. Yes it is performed as a 'memory' stunt but it does involve memorising a lot of numeric data.

It basically involves attaching specific numbers as key figures to the days of the week and to the months of the year. If it was just one number to connect to each of them then a simple link for each would be fine. Invariably when it comes to algorithm's like this and the variations around it, that is not the case. You can create a journey based around its origin. For example, the key figures for the days of the week I looked at my life for specific things that I did on a Monday or specific things for a Tuesday and built the stories around this. The reason being that whenever I completed these tasks in the real world then I would get a free top up of the information needed whenever and wherever I went as the 'links' on my journey would be there each time. A storage of information that is directly linked to the information needed and filed in a very organised way that is needed to complete the task of figuring out the day for any day of the week.

To put this into a grander context, if you are working a case you observe information concerning people, the business they all work for, the cars involved in commutes and arrivals to work, the placement of staff on a particular floor. To collect this all in one journey has the potentiality to conflate parts of the information just because it is so vast and technical in its differences. We can use the specific creation of journeys to separate out this information and store it organically. When you have developed your awareness of journey creation you can ask yourself *'What do you think of in your life that reminds you of a mass of people?'* For me this would be a stadium event of any kind that I have been to. A gig, theatre show, anything. From there I immediately have directions from the entrance to the ticket stalls, to the bathroom, to cafe, to my seat, to the bar. Using this method would allow me to categorise this information as I went.

The belief, rightly or wrongly, that the information can just be added to or retrieved from a palace of Sherlockian magnitude is, I am sorry to say, an unnecessary hindrance. A brake in your ability to observe and memorise as much as is needed to successfully navigate a situation that you are involved in. The grandiose palace has a multitude of uses but when pressure and time are of the essence,

that is not one of them. This is a necessary reflex to build for creating a natural grasp of as much information in the area as you possibly can. Without affecting your cognitive load and therefore performance.

With this next example this is merely an exercise in journey creation and not observation of all of the information. However, parameters of the exercise first. Watch the video in full once and only once. It is a 360 degree video as well just so you know that you can turn the screen to find out more and more information. The requirements would be for you to come away with information regarding the volume of people there, where they were going, what they were doing, who was wearing what, time of day, location and anything else you can provide on top of this. Only thing is, you don't know where you are going to see this information and in what order. How are you going to sort it all through? Use this to try and devise some organic journeys that are prompted by the details in your prefrontal cortex.

What you are building with this is a capability to navigate large amounts of data in pressured situations. The journey title itself will now act as the catalyst link for you to maintain these details throughout the course of your day. The combination of methods in this way will facilitate a growth in your observational capabilities. Meaning you can spend more of your focus on the details. After all, details matter! This method of journey creation will mean that a creation of a Sherlockian memory palace will be easier, by no means easy, easier as a result. We will get to that shortly though.

For now there is one thing I would like you to consider. A point that one could argue should belong in the mindset chapter. As this directly concerns memory and observation I am placing it here for you. You WILL miss things. It is quite simply not possible for you to see and observe absolutely everything. Even when you account for your peripherals. This will be something that you will need to get used to. It is something that will tax the strength of your capacity to stay in the required mindset to be able to focus to the best of your abilities at that time. To say that your efficacy is predicated on your capability to notice and capitalise on the information that is contained around you whilst being ok with the fact that you will miss things sounds like an oxymoron right? Yet this is something that you will need to become aware of and through exposure and experience this is something that you will need to develop.

In addition to this, when thinking of the speed with which real life can occur, there may be an issue in which you are thinking words to the effect of 'well which method should I use and when?' When you have the benefit of time and foresight to be able to apply this to the information being thrown at you then this is something that you can entertain. However, when things are simply happening thick and fast around, this is not always possible. I am reminded of the words of a very important person for this particular quandary:

"A good martial artist does not become tense, but ready. Not thinking, yet not dreaming. Ready for whatever may come. When the opponent expands, I contract; and when he contracts, I expand. And when there is an opportunity, "I" do not hit, "it" hits all by itself."
Bruce Lee

You will need to take the active steps to develop each of these methods to such a degree that they can happen at the drop of a hat. All this is happening within full control of yourself and your cognitive capabilities. It is your time spent second guessing which method is best or what you should use that will stop the strength of the retention being what it should be. Like a great motivational video (great in my opinion anyway) once said ,"Stop thinking and just do!!"

So long as you have the information with you in your head. You can file it away as needed at a time that is best suited by the situation and/or the requirements of the scenario. If you are taking time to decide the method when you should be observing then in the words of a martial artist, you are reacting and not acting. In which case you are already on the back foot.

A brief thesis on something massive

It seems to me that the nature of a memory palace has been somewhat mythologised over the last decade or so thanks largely to the way that this has been depicted in the media. As well as some of the bold claims that have been made by charlatans online about what their memories and cerebral skills can do. I mean, we all saw the nonsense of the speed-reader claiming to read a full book in a few seconds right?! If you haven't then please google this and brace your stomach for some extensive laughter! Just to be clear in terms of the terminology, when I say a memory palace I mean a literal housing unit for all of the information I want to store in there. A mental lukasa if you will - don't worry, we'll get there.

There are a great many people that seem to be labouring under the misapprehension that the purpose of the memory palace is to be full, so that indeed you will never forget anything. It seems to me that the purpose of a memory palace is for it to be empty. Crazy right? Let me explain.

The memory palace in short is a housing unit for potentially a lot of data. What we know of consolidation is that the more you use a piece of information, the less and less it becomes something that you have to recall and moves into being something that you just know. With this in mind, you don't need to have some extensive palatial space that is worthy of the ancient Greeks. You can use a house and just make sure everything is filed correctly and when you have used the information from somewhere to such a degree that the mnemonics are not needed then you can redecorate and kick the information out in favour of new stuff. The size of your palace will directly correlate to the size of the information you have to store.

My point in telling you this is that if a palace is something you have a utilitarian requirement for then by all means develop it. It has helped me no end of times over the years. However please don't conflate the development of this with being enamoured with the folklore behind it. It may wind up being a giant waste of your time otherwise. The information that you store should be directly related to how much you intend to use it or at the very least, have an idea as to how it is that it will be used.

Pre-Memory Prehistoric, Pre-most things

The entire purpose of the next few pieces of information is for you to understand that the 'memory techniques' that can be used, go far beyond the mere simplicity of mnemonics. In terms of anything I have to tell you about it would come from my experience of using these and how they relate to the specifics of the personal way I think about things in relation to the application of learnt material. If these end up being something of interest for you then you must set this book down and go and source all that you can by Lynne Kelly. Particularly her incredible books *The Memory Code* and *Memory Craft*.

For me, this has been the single most enjoyable experience of memory work and when I discovered this years ago it opened up so many other areas for me to explore. It made the notion of memory work a full body experience. So again, this is experiential information and while it might be connected on the surface to studies/books/courses that I have consumed this is only in terms of my use of this. With that in mind, let's begin.

Songlines

Also known as a Dreaming track, they really gave me the opportunity to indulge my flamboyance a bit. Originally used to track paths across the land and skies. The paths of the song lines are recorded in traditional songs, stories, dance, and painting. So in essence, every time these tribes were to complete one of their songs they would be revivifying huge stacks of data regarding journeys through lands that had no sat navs or sign posts and where they would have to make sure that food could be naturally sourced and all through a non-literate world. So what does that mean for us when we use these things nowadays? We are all different and yes the myriad of methods may work for some people but not for all. So we could be better cognitively equipped if we had things like this at our disposal.

To create a song line you can approach this in a similar way to the basic creation of a memory palace or a journey. Take a song that you know well and have a reasonable emotive connection with....

"But Ben I don't want to change my favourite song in the world, I like it how it is."

That's the usual sentence that my students come out with at this stage. To which my answer is always words to the effect of *'Well don't then."*

There are more than enough songs in the world to choose from. You just need to know it well enough that you could sing it all to yourself. Even if I made you choose your all-time favourite song in the world then through the act of consolidation of the data you use in your new song line, the lyrics would be freed up after use and it would return to normal because of how much it has been used.

Here is the way I used it. I stored the London Underground system on the Muse album Origin of Symmetry. I have been a big Muse fan for years and I know most of their catalogue by heart anyway. So let's take one of the stations and 10 of its stops. I will be using their song Newborn as a guide for this so if you don't know the song and you want to follow along properly then please google it and come back.

Here are 10 stops on the Victoria line:
1. Brixton
2. Stockwell
3. Vauxhall
4. Pimlico
5. Victoria
6. Green Park
7. Oxford Circus
8. Warren Street
9. Euston Street
10. King's Cross St Pancras

Job one is to begin thinking about the Mnemonic conversions you can use here, or the images that the words themselves conjure up. This will make the lyrics easier to manage in a moment. Here are some ideas for you:
1. Bricks, a ton of bricks, Brixton is the name of Idris Elba's Character in Hobbs and Shaw
2. A well-stocked shelf, a wishing well full of beef stock,
3. The car brand, a hall filled with foxes
4. Someone forgot how to pronounce Pimsleur, someone drinking Pimm's in a limo (Limousine)
5. Queen Victoria, Niki Minaj's real name, Victoria wood

6. Little green men at the park, a park of jealousy, a park that is literally made of dollar bills
7. The Kingsman (from the film of the same name) at the circus. Their saying was 'Oxford's not brogues'.
8. Rabbits crossing the street to go home. Rabbits live in a warren. Warren Buffet, Warren Beatty, Warren brown
9. Astronauts in peril 'Euston we have a problem'.
10. Any infamous king that you know but give them diabetes

Then what you do is look at the lyrics of the song you are looking to use and follow along with the cadence and syllable usage to make a new song out of the images you have created. Here are the lyrics to the first verse of Newborn.

Link it to the world
Link it to yourself
Stretch it like a birth squeeze
The love for what you hide
The bitterness inside
Is growing like the newborn
When you've seen, seen
Too much too young, young
Soulless is everywhere

Stay with me as the fun can really start now. I have then made this song read like this:

Brixton stocks the shelves

Well with foxes from the hall
Pimms in a Limo with the Queen
Green men are at the park
Kingsmen's favourite shoes
Rabbits are going home
Spacemen having problems
King Charles has type 2 diabetes

In an effort to provide full and well-rounded understanding to the change here, this QR code above is me singing the application. Brace yourself as I cannot sing at all. I don't mind singing but it will not sound pleasant. Once you have this method down, there is no end to the creative ways that you would  be able to store quite a lot of information. The added bonus is in the process of consolidation you get to enjoy singing along to some music you enjoy but learning as you go. However if you are anything like me this will entail you screeching along to songs you enjoy whilst playing air drums on your car steering wheel and hoping that the airbag doesn't burst forward.

Memory Boards

Another practice derived from generations past and yet we can still see echoes of this existing today. Particularly with reference to UK culture. I am not as aware of its existence globally; a few places around the world for sure but not everywhere. Children learn through playing and creation. Creating collages from moments in history, or even a diorama or 2 being made to commemorate some important literature that is the current topic at the time. I am looking at you Lisa Simpson and the Tell Tale Heart. Put short, this is another creative way for us to be able to inhabit the information that we need to memorise. Sadly though this is something that we tend to lose as adults. Being the obsessive flamboyant dork that I am, I am doing what I can to popularise these methods as much as possible.

Lukasas and Tjurungas are examples of memory boards. Lukasas are closely associated with the history of the Luba kingdom. No-one could be moved into office without first becoming a member of the Bambudye society, and the ruler of the Luba kingdom held the highest ranking Bambudye title. Traditionally speaking, they were or rather, they are hourglass shaped bits of wood with all manner of jewels and buttons and brightly coloured things attached to them in very specific ways to the board's creator. The colours and patterns of beads or ideograms serve to stimulate the recollection of important people, places, things, relationships and events as court historians narrate the origins of Luba authority. Tjurungas are stone or wooden objects possessed by private or group owners together with the legends, chants, and ceremonies associated with them. The use of them prompts the specific chants to be completed and the information 'topped up' as a result.

For you and me, we can get as creative with this as we want. It would be all about specifically how the board relates to the material and how you connect to it in general. When I wanted to create mine I wanted it specifically for memorising dog breeds. Namely the vital statistics and visuals that go along with each individual breed. So when I looked around for pieces of wood I was going to use to experiment with adding all of my brightly coloured things to, I first looked at bits of wood. To assess their size and ease of their use. I found some old bits of timber that I had originally used to make some gym equipment with. As luck would have it, the first dog on my list (that was in no special order) was a Dachshund - more commonly known as a sausage dog.

The first bit I saw on the timber with all of the varying degrees of brown, actually looked like a little sausage dog. Albeit longer and a bit thinner in the proportions but a Dachshund all the same. So I sent all of my crafty add ons back and set about the bits of wood with a very sharp knife and lots of patience so as not to cut myself and crafted my Memory board rather than added to it. Depending on your country of origin there are a different number of recognised breeds but on a global scale there are around 360 breeds of dogs. On my 2 bits of wood I have 150 species on there but with each species, comes with it a laundry list of details.

Now here's the thing, just as I imagine it is possible for you to tell me what your house is decorated like in intricate detail, given enough time with your memory board you will be able to do the same. So much so that the board itself would become surplus to requirements. This can then be added to your palace in your head and get rid of the boards if you don't want them lying around the house. Or if you are anything like my wife, you want to use them for axe throwing practice.

These are just 2 methods that are arguably not as well-known as some of the others in print already, however, should these be of interest to you then please go and immerse yourself in anything Lynne Kelly says or does. She is a font of knowledge well worth drinking from. I have experimented with others, for example who the Inuits would tie knots in specific bits of rope is also very interesting but these are the 2 methods that I have spent lots of time with so I give to you my experience in the hopes that it will inspire something within you.

Thus concludes our upgrade on memory work from the last time we looked at this together. I do hope that it awakens something within you. The main points of note are that if you were looking for something to help you with competition memory methods then this, aint that. I also wanted to point you towards some of the lesser spoken about vehicles of using memory methods that in my opinion should be looked at in much more detail. I look forward to hearing about how all of you get on.

Facing the facts

'The face is like the penis! And this is what he meant in that the face has, to a large extent, a mind of its own. Often, some little part of a suppressed emotion leaks out.' - Silvan Tomkins

Not that I have much support for the above as a frame of reference for understanding the face. I heard it referenced in an episode of Elementary and thought that it would be a pithy quotation to use in relation to how one would understand the movements of the face in relation to what people are saying, thinking and feeling. When it comes to the work in this area, it is long and expansive and, arguably most importantly, is still underway. There is a lot of bullshit that is peddled around what 'face reading' is capable of and what it is not capable of doing. Suffice to say that if you ascribe to the Ekman view of paying attention to the briefest of facial twitches and how this is a direct link to what is specifically going on in people's heads then you will need a re-education. Let's call a spade a spade as well, when the first version of The Monographs was being written I had yet to receive the proper education around this topic. I was fully engaged in the 'buy and read' everything phase and had not taken into account that purely using someone's bibliography for additional research is an extended confirmation bias. Since that time, a few short months after its release, I received the proper information around this.

In terms of understanding someone's emotional responses to something, there will be no hard and fast rule of anything where *this* means *that* as a direct result of something that you have seen or noticed. People and behaviour in general, simply does not work that way. It may provide you with an idea or an insight into something. The only way you are going to know anything for sure though is by using the observations you have made as well as the connected data that it leads to in order to validate, dismiss or clarify your hypotheses at that time. There is no world where the mere twitch of an eye brow can reveal something about an individual with regard to their deception levels or not. So where does that leave us? What can we learn about the face when 'reading' someone else in the moment.

When we look at the work of Dr Lisa Feldman Barrett this provides us with more of a direct insight into how emotions are made and therefore the displays that we would individually use to demonstrate them. If I may paraphrase a part of this work here and so we can have a grounding in how the rest of this chapter is going to go; the things that make me happy are down to my experiences and the connected situations that led to me actually experiencing them. The same items for someone in Australia or for someone in the middle of the jungle would provide an entirely different reaction and therefore presentation by virtue of this huge change in circumstances.

Think of it like this, I love (understatement of the century) chocolate chip cookies. Consuming these makes me happy. My positivity will be different if I am eating cookies because I am hungry or because I am breaking my diet, maybe even because they were a gift. I may bare my teeth in a smile because someone is giving me a gift of something I enjoy, yet the smile may be invisible when eating these purely because I am hungry and yet I would classify myself as happy in every scenario. So how can we look at the face in such a way that we can get some kind of content that we can act upon. Whether you look at Freudian Hydraulic's or the anecdotal insights of your brain being responsible for regulating your body and that being the reason behind its evolution, emotions take a toll on you. Whatever emotion it is that you experience, if you experience it to a heightened degree or for an extended period then emotions take their toll on you. Physically and mentally affecting us all as a result in some way. There is an expenditure of energy towards emotions that we as humans will rationalise in the moment as to whether or not we should be feeling it and the degree to which we should be feeling it as well.

Before we get into it I should point a few things out. This is my work in an area that is rife with bold claims. I looked for things that could not be refuted and how I could use them to gain insight into someone else. This takes stock of anatomical knowledge and research, critical thinking techniques and connected elements. This is a system that can be put to work with the people that you meet. I will only tell you about what I have taught based on the successes of the thousands of people I have taught it to. However, I am not claiming it to be perfect. If there is someone out there that knows something that would change how I look at the topics in this chapter then I absolutely want to know so that the techniques can be refined. So, with that in mind, let's do this.

Set in Stone

The face is designed to move in very specific ways. For the majority of people, the cheeks, eyebrows, the lips and eyelids as well as everything else have grown to move in one way. This is how anatomy text books around the world teach the same information. The size, shape, colour and position of the muscles, tissue and everything else will be the differing elements that give us our looks. The path, direction, channel or whatever other synonym you would like to use would remain the singular thing that we can work with here. This is one of the things, I believe, that gave credence to the whole 'universality of emotional displays' epidemic. I have never seen that written anywhere though it's just a thought I took from Darwin's books.

The only differences, if we were to be a little semantic about the details, would be as a result of some sort of trauma, illness, procedure or a combination of the 3. So what I have to work with at this stage is a known direction of the way muscles move in the face and a small subset of known interferences to that organic movement. This can mean that in the early stages of 'reading' a face I can know if I am dealing with a finite niche area of information that has compensated in some way when showing some form of emotional range or that they will display it as their own experiences would dictate that it should be displayed. Now this all sounds like a fancy way of not really saying a great deal but I am only interested at this moment in where the facts are within the face that I can work with. This initial realisation will make a great starting point. Others will advise that there is no need to learn about the muscles of the face and which way they are anatomically supposed to move. I have found a great deal of success in this area with understanding the kind of face I am looking at. To be naturally inhibited or to be inhibited by some external force so to speak.

Cultural Differences

As the emotions we choose to display and how we choose to display them can be described as a culmination of our experience within this wide ranging area, the displays that are attributed to something positive like being happy for an English person would likely be very different to someone who lives in Guadalajara. Sure, you may see a smile and think that it is the same thing that functions in the same way as everyone and everything else but this is a misnomer.

'They did not observe full smiles on photos until 1920; however, by 1970 approx. 60% of the men and 80% of the women showed a partial or complete smile. In both studies gender differences emerged: women smiled more than men. '

Hess, Ursula, Martin G. Beaupré, and Nicole Cheung. "Who to whom and why–cultural differences and similarities in the function of smiles." *An empirical reflection on the smile* 4 (2002): 187.

There are gender differences of all sorts, cultural differences, smiles when happy, sad, annoyed, secretive, envious, embarrassed about eating all of the cookies in the house and a whole heap more. Smiling can be considered a form of social currency in some areas of the western world and a sign of weakness in some areas of the eastern. So what is my point in telling you all of this?

As someone who is on the road to being able to understand someone from what we observe, we can take a great deal of insight from learning about culture and the differing interpretations of the exact same thing therein. Think of it this way; there have been 15 different versions of the TV Show 'The Office' that have been made around the world. Within that 15 I am including the original and the American version as well. A show based pretty much on the exact same thing and with many similar characters. You will be able to see the lead in each, display the same or similar emotions and experiences but how this is changed through the culture of that part of the world.

For example, something I noticed amongst my friends, so take this with the biggest pinch of salt if you would like, is the difference between the smiles of those in the UK or the USA and those in Eastern Europe. I have some friends in Serbia, Poland and Moldova that smile with the most action in the cheeks and the ears. It is like someone has stretched their Buccinators back in a line towards their eyes. I see them do it just as I do the people in the local stores in the area. Whereas over here and in the states there is much more action in the eyes and the ears barely move, if at all. Does that mean one person is happy and the other is not? Absolutely not! It just indicates that there are cultural differences when it comes to the expression of the same thing.

What we have before us is an avenue of continued research and exploration that we can use to help shape the accuracy of our observations. If there is a part of the world I am not that familiar with then it becomes up to me to make myself familiar. As a lovely second hand treat this will also improve my understanding and critical thinking of people that could have any projected biases pushed on to them that don't need to. If your usual run of expressions and displays that you are used to is very animated and full of energy then should you come across someone that is the very opposite of this then you might unwittingly assume that they are cold or grumpy in some form. It may just be that their cultural experience is more understated than your own. As such you will have a wider pool of information to pull from.

Emotional language

We covered a lot of things within the face topic in the first version and so I am only interested in doing my best to build on the information that is available for you. With that said, as we are looking at the displays of the face and their relationship towards a felt state then we can also look at the way someone is able to describe the emotions that either they or others feel.

When I read *The Emotions of Normal People* by William Moulton Marston I thought it was awesome. In that, I thought it was hilarious. What even is a normal person anyway?! How could I rationally explain to William that I was pissed off at a sandwich for not tasting as good as I thought it would because I was hungry?! Describing my feelings in relation to food would not make a great deal of sense on the surface and yet it was very real to me. The language I use would be a link to be able to understand how nuanced I consider my own feelings to be.

When I was a personal trainer there would be 1 or 2 of my clients who would reference their struggles with snacking as making them feel 'sad'. My response was always words to the effect of 'Are you?' Are they actually sad is an important distinction to make in their understanding of the moments they are experiencing. When I got them to look at this in more detail they diagnosed these moments as reactions to stress, boredom, guilt, nerves and even excitement. Within this simple diagnosis they gave themselves more self-awareness of the changing moments around their snacking to be able to take an active step in changing what they do. For someone to frown and claim they are sad, compared to someone crying and saying they are gutted are 2 very different things. This granularity will allow further understanding of their experience during the movements of the face. This is an idea I took from Brene Brown's work in emotional granularity. Just because someone says they are gutted doesn't mean they actually are, it simply means that their experience is more nuanced in that moment. Listen to the language someone uses to describe their experience.

Time Matters

This is something that could go into a chapter referencing deception detection however I am choosing to keep it within this chapter because it has more to do with the face than it does the complicated and complex notion of 'lie detection'. The length of time it takes for an expression to fade is indicative of its genuine connection. If you were to laugh in response to a joke of some sort and then immediately change your face to a stern expression, this would indicate a dichotomy in terms of why the laugh might not be real. For a laugh to vanish would indicate that it was not felt. If you look at *The Anatomy of Laughter by Toby Garfitt* we have an understanding that laughter is a complete take-over of your body and cognitive capabilities. For this to then vanish would indicate that it wasn't felt or would be seen as being impeded by very tight and stern cheeks.

For genuine emotions to vanish under utilitarian control of the face would require some impressive, almost sociopathic level of control. This is the same of virtually all emotions. The onset can be slow building but in most circumstances, for the presentation of the visible detail to immediately change or vanish would indicate that it wasn't truly felt. The most obvious example is 'the awkward laugh'. This is something that leaks out during moments of nerves and/or anxiety. I believe that all of us would agree that this particular expression isn't a real laugh in terms of being a release of positivity. The disappearance of the movement is the key to breaking this down.

To sum up, as we covered things like earrings and shaving in the first edition, we are not going to go over this again here. For what we are concerned with for this chapter in isolation it is to take note of the fact that in terms of a majority, the face is designed to move in very specific ways. This changes through the lens of the culture that they are developed in and can be altered by some form of external involvement through disease, trauma and/or surgery. Fake expressions evaporate whereas the genuinely felt ones can linger.

Let's use this as an example to illustrate the topics we have covered within this chapter. This will take into account the following citation:

'Jack, R. E., Sun, W., Delis, I., Garrod, O. G. B., & Schyns, P. G. (2016). Four not six: Revealing culturally common facial expressions of emotion. Journal of Experimental Psychology: General, 145(6), 708–730'

Humans use complex facial expressions to communicate a diverse range of emotions, and there has been a long-standing debate on whether these expressions are universal across cultures or culture-specific. Recent research suggests that there are four latent and culturally common facial expression patterns that each communicate specific combinations of valence, arousal, and dominance. These findings have direct implications for emotion communication, social psychology, cognitive neuroscience, and social robotics. The widely held view that 6 facial expression patterns are universal has been challenged by this research, instead suggesting 4 latent expressive patterns. This has important implications for understanding cross-cultural communication of emotions. Changing the understanding of the game once again, shocking right?...

What we then see as a sub section of this research is the experimental differences in smiling between even similar cultures. Recent research from Social Psychologists such as Abigail Marsh suggests that nonverbal accents can reveal cultural identification through emotion expressions. People from different cultures perceive emotions conveyed by facial expressions differently, with Chinese participants relying more on the eyes and Western Caucasians relying more on the eyebrows and mouth. Emotion expressions can reveal cultural accents, as the intensity of happiness expression aligns with different cultural ideals of excited versus calm happiness. Despite cultural differences, people from different cultures share about 70% of the facial expressions used in response to different social and emotional situations. She has shown that people could tell whether someone was Japanese or Japanese American (in other words, which culture they belonged to) from photos of their faces.

In essence, what I am saying is, though spotting micro expressions may be a fun intellectual flex, their reliability is far from what Cal Lightman would have you believe that it is.

Deceptively Obvious Facts

"No man has a good enough memory to be a successful liar." - Abraham Lincoln

This could be one of those chapters that would really infuriate me to write or it would excite me at the prospect of trying to burst the bubble that mass media and misinformation has produced around the human efficacy with lie detection. Let's see how I get on. Maybe you could consider it a personal deductive challenge to try and figure out which side of the line I fall on as you read this.

In terms of a generalised view of the popular information that is out there regarding lie detection there seems to be the idea that you can apply a mathematical idea to it, spotting a specific number of a certain tells, the old deviation from the baseline ruse, hidden micro expressions and behavioural changes. In short, nope. Though that may be more of a colloquial answer than anything else. For anyone that listens to The Deductionist Podcast you will be well aware of my proclivity for the more adult descriptions. However, let's try and keep this as fair as possible. There is no hard and fast rule of spotting a lie. There is no step by step element or a formula that you can apply. Humans would need to work with a vast amount of consistent predictability for this to be the case. Nobody seems to step back a step further and address why 'Lie detection' is even a topic that is taught. I mean I totally understand why it is a field of research but to be taught is something else altogether.

To look for lies is to immediately bias what you are seeing anyway. It is a little like walking into the conversations you have with the expected understanding that someone is going to lie to you. Your conversational capability is immediately harmed. The potential for you to misinterpret every Freudian slip, gestural retreat or arm cross as signalling deception goes up as a result. Instead, if you think of lying as something that may come up. Some details that may not make sense within the others that have been spoken, then this will make you more receptive to those changes as and when they occur. You need to have all of the information available first before you are equipped to decide truth from lie, fact from fiction and even then it is not anything that is a definitive response. Like a binary answer to a question. There is something my friend and colleague Jim Wenzel states about his encounters within Policing and the world of security in general. You can validate, dismiss or clarify details the more that a conversation unfurls.

To spot a lie is by virtue of exploration. It is not the result of a recipe that you apply. It can't be. Where are the formulas that account for the lie's I have spotted by Virtue of an errant smell or knowing the location of something that I am being told is somewhere else. The answer is, there aren't any. The available data at the moment seems to rely close to completely, on looking at humans. We should all know from having interacted with humans in some form or another for however long you have been alive, that they are unreliable at best. At worst some people aren't in tune enough with their own data stream enough to know when they are lying and when they are not.

Whereas you can take stock of a lot of information from a human being in any particular moment. The second you start to 'look for lies' you have somewhat tipped your hand. This prevents us from being as present and in the moment of observing as you could be because you are looking at the information in front of you through a lens of expectation. So what can we talk about here that would help you on your journey to be able to spot them as and when they occur. It is a fiendishly simple thing to say but insanely complex task to carry out. It is the reason why this has been printed on my business cards for years....OBSERVE EVERYTHING.

To be clear this is simply my approach and my teachings based on the years of failing, trial and error, success rates and purposeful challenges that I have set myself. This should, I hope, not detract from your understanding of its efficacy but more to measure your expectations accordingly. If it is that you are looking for ways to be able to look at people, watch a few movements and know categorically if they are telling the truth or not then you need another book by someone who is prepared to lie to you. Ironic no? So let's start as we mean to go on and bust a few fallacies.

I Would Never Lie To You....

We have probably all heard words to this effect from someone at some point in our lives. We accept this as true and those who state that well, you could lie to me, are pasted as neurotic in some way. These are the facts. Everyone has the capacity to lie to everyone else. A few mental health conditions are the exceptions but in general terms this is true. Yet someone who has millions of followers on whatever social media platform is currently the focus is now saying 'With these 10 steps you can become a Human Lie Detector' and we immediately accept this as true. It's on the internet so it must be true, mustn't it?

If I had a pound for every time...no...if I had a penny for every time I have heard or come across something like this then I would be just as rich as if I kept the pound as the focus within the analogy. It is a conversation that goes something like this:

Person on line: *Well they said that this was the way I could guarantee that I can spot lies*

Ben: *What makes you think that is the case?*

Person on line: *Well they are the number 1 body language expert*

Ben: *Given that there are no competitions to decide that. Who decided they were?*

Person on line: *Well, they have 500,000 twitter followers*

Ben: *Understood. So Justin Bieber is the best musician in the world then?*

Person on line: *No. What do you mean?*

Ben: Well he has the most twitter followers in music

I have no gripe with anything other than with the fact that popularity is used as a measure for critical thought around a topic. That can't be the case. I would encourage everyone to review the available work of Vincent Denault. A man that is seemingly fighting a 1 man war against misinformation. The answer to being to spot lies does not use a 1 size fits all methodology, again it can't. Humans don't all think and act in the same way. We are looking for ways to be able to do this using one method when it seems to me that the answer lies somewhere in the middle of the spectrum. This immediately makes people uncomfortable but having an arsenal of things that we can choose from is going to make sure that we are better suited for each new situation that arises.

So when it comes to Ekman's work we can start by acknowledging that it is flawed and has never been properly reviewed (to the best of my knowledge), Polygraphs we covered in the first edition as well. baselining, any article that tries to contain lie detection to 10 or even 110 points and anything related to this. If these are something you are placing your faith in then please, I urge you for the sake of your effectiveness, think bigger. If I may be allowed to continue the urging to present you with something that may be worthwhile to you then please look into the world of Cognitive Load Theory.

Cognitive Load Theory (CLT) is an instructional design theory that focuses on how our brains process and store information. According to CLT, human beings have a limited capacity for working memory. When presented with information that exceeds this capacity, learning becomes difficult. Effective learning occurs when individuals allocate an optimal amount of cognitive resources and consider the limitations of working memory. Brain activity changes reflect effortful cognition, and neural efficiency is linked to cognitive demands and measures cognitive load. Working memory is crucial for higher-order cognitive activities and is correlated with fluid intelligence. Failures in task learning happen when task demands exceed capacity or when mental resources are not allocated adequately. Techniques for objectively assessing cognitive load are needed to quantify training efficiency, but relying solely on subjective introspection can be problematic.

This is something that lie spotters have attempted to take advantage of for years and yet it is something that the lie spotter themselves should be well aware of as well. They would be just as at risk of its pitfalls as someone who is trying to lie. As someone who is trying to observe a person there is so much to take stock of, so much to see, and so much to process. The cognitive load that you truly have to bear is huge! This is why we should spend much of our time training. This would take the form of reading, researching, practising and pressurising ourselves in order to try and combat the effects of CLT on us. The more information we have to make use of when looking at a situation that we need to observe then the better equipped we will be to be able to make an effective read of the situation.

To illustrate the considerations with an example, I will be purposefully sparse on the details, lest I get into trouble. I saw an interview that was being taken outside. The woman in question was talking about something that she claimed was troubling her quite a lot. The therapist that was leading the discussion was taken in by the situation as it resonated with details from her past too. The woman in question had hay fever. I asked the therapist to consider the wind as an effect on the eyes. Not merely something that supports her growing connection to the woman being interviewed. She was hesitant. So I acted as someone with no stake in the matter and merely offered a Clarityn. For those that don't know what this is, it is hay fever medicine here in the UK. She took it from me graciously and about 20 minutes later her eyes were back to normal and her emotional displays didn't seem as emotional as they initially did to the therapist.

The therapist and I spoke about it after and I just said that I noticed that you were at risk of not seeing the information that you needed to see because your objectivity had been robbed as a result of the cognitive load you were bearing. The rest of the interview was carried out with the woman in question in as standard a manner as is possible.

My point in telling you all of this is that a lie can come from anywhere and at any time. The more responsive you are to all of the information that is going on around you including the behaviour you are seeing then you will stand better odds of being able to separate fact from fiction. This will never be in a totalitarian black and white way unless the lies are part of a training game that you are playing. Of which there are many and we will go into a couple shortly for you to play.

The main port of call as a take away from this chapter is to explore as many avenues as you are able to without compromising your effectiveness in the moment. This will ultimately make sure that whatever information you end up with at the end is as direct as it can be. Cognitive Load theory and pushing my capabilities with this forms a big part of all of my training. In essence it works like most physical training. If I struggle to do 5 pull ups then I aren't going to try and demonstrate my capacity to do 7 to others until that is something that

I can comfortably achieve. With this in mind you should not be looking to actively spot lies until you have reached some kind of verifiable competency in being able to track multiple sources of information. This can be anything from my audio and listening games from the first edition to trying to study with the world going on around you. The directions of pushing this will be idiosyncratic to you but the corollaries of being able to bear a higher cognitive load the more you practise will be there for all to take.

Lying is not about 1 single thing, or a particular set of skills if you will allow me to paraphrase. It is about many, it is about everything that is going on in a moment where lies would be possible. For example, are you aware of how many different kinds of lies there are? Not something many consider in this area. It is apparently just down to one or the other. Yet in the simple acknowledgement of this distinction it can allow us a grander insight as we can start to look at something more verifiable from a contextual angle, motivation.

The following is my summation of the available data:

Error
If I told you my trainers cost me £120 when in fact I stole them, then you told someone else that I paid £120 for my trainers then you have told a lie in error. Close to omission but not 100% the same.

Omission
Leaving out the all-important pieces to a particular puzzle. For instance, if a person knew that their friend's partner was cheating but

chose not to tell their friend, that would be a lie of omission.

Denial
Denial occurs when someone tells another or themselves that they don't know the truth. More often than not this is done under the guise of protecting someone else from harm. This is very close to the example given above but differs in the motivation.

Falsification
Falsifying information is the term used to describe a lie or story which occurs in an attempt to get more attention or sympathy, or to intentionally hurt another person. Someone who values the pity they get from others and at the top end of the spectrum would be something like Munchausen's.

Misinterpretation
Misinterpretation is when someone misinterprets something that occurred and shares this information with others. You will find this in a lot of the Pseudoscience peddled about Body Language in popular media.

Bold-Faced Lie
A bold-faced lie happens when someone tells a lie that everyone knows is a lie. This should be obvious. If you know something and then actively say something else then this would be the bold faced lie. *I did not have sexual relations with that woman* for example.

White Lie

A white lie is when someone tells another person a lie that is harmless. The classic trope is a wife asking her husband, does my bum look big in this and the husband saying no, not at all. Even when he can see that, that is simply not the case.

Exaggeration

Most stories that nervous guys in bars tell or even narcissists for that matter fall victim to this type of claim. The show off business exec that claims he could buy a helicopter on a whim or the drunk guy at the end of the bar that claims he once beat up 10 guys in a fight when it was just the one.

Pathological Lying

Pathological lying happens when people constantly tell lies for no apparent reason. Those who are known to be pathological liars can often not be trusted. Those people who claim that every politician falls into this category would be close to being at risk of not being able to bear the cognitive load of their own biases.

Pathological lying, also known as pseudologia fantastica, is a condition characterised by compulsive lying and fabricating stories without a clear motive. It is not typically associated with specific medical conditions, but rather considered a symptom or behaviour associated with certain psychiatric disorders. Antisocial Personality Disorder, Narcissistic Personality Disorder, Borderline Personality Disorder, Histrionic Personality Disorder, Bipolar Disorder, Factitious

Disorder, Substance Use Disorders (particularly when lying is associated with obtaining drugs or concealing use.)

I would like you not to forget that there is a stigma attached to lying. You very often hear things like 'You dirty liar' and words to that effect on a colloquial level. Throughout most cultures and societies we are engineered to know and understand lying is wrong and for someone to be caught in a lie is to acknowledge in some way that you have the capacity for wrongdoing. The reason behind why some of the available research goes into behavioural leakage. The human's connection to something they feel to be wrong and so the information leaks out. This is very often not the case with the aforementioned disorders. To pathologically lie is to bring that element of saying something that 'isn't' without any internal distress into your behavioural make up. The credit we give to actors in this vein is because nobody is directly hurt as a result.

Minimization

Using your words to do the best to minimise the effects that you caused that everyone else would be able to see. One of the most famous examples of a lie where someone tried to minimise the effects of what they did is the Watergate scandal. During the Watergate scandal in the 1970s, President Richard Nixon and his administration attempted to cover up their involvement in the break-in at the Democratic National Committee headquarters. They lied to the public, the media, and investigators in an effort to downplay their role and minimise the impact of their actions. Ultimately, their lies were exposed, and Nixon was forced to resign from the presidency. This example highlights the consequences of attempting to minimise the effects of a lie.

With this many different options for the 'liar' to take, can we really just say it is about right and wrong, good and bad. Considering prevarication as more of a spectrum than anything else would allow us to gain a more direct insight into motivation for the statements that are made during this time. With all of this in mind, why do people even bother trying to separate someone's stories into fact and fiction? Even when there is such a high possibility of failure. Such a high probability of misdiagnosis. The answer to this can only be a personal opinion and it is inherently a simple one. It is because it is a fascination and a belief that to understand when someone lies is to understand them truly. What someone would lie about is to know where their perception of their deep secrets lie. If I were going to lie to you about how much I weigh, it would directly indicate some belief that I have about myself about the significance of what that number is and its relation to my life.

How can we sum this up then for one's ability to 'spot lies'. First of all the topic could never be covered in a simple chapter. Let alone a simple book for that matter. We have, I hope, gone some way to helping you to understand what it actually is to catch a lie. The bullet points from the chapter as your take away are as follows:

- Observe everything
- Everyone has the capacity to lie
- Question your observations

- Pay attention to the degree of cognitive load that you can take
- Acknowledge the cognitive load that others can bear
- Be aware of the variations to a simple lie

The best of luck with all of your pursuits. Whether they be as honestly deceptive as a performance or the humble restraint of a white lie.

"No legacy is so rich as honesty." - William Shakespeare

Occupational Observations

'Education never ends, Watson. It is a series of lessons with the greatest for the last.'
Sherlock Holmes - The Red Circle

My work in this area remains remarkably simple when compared to the first edition. It is something that will be an ongoing factor of my research and continuous editions to my memory palace. This is still arguably one of the most repeated questions I am asked. It no doubt stems from people's fascination with the depiction of Sherlock Holmes in the media and the misunderstanding of its translation to the world. The actions of being able to look at someone and deduce what they did for a living could be described as an oxymoron. On the one hand you just have to have a familiarity with the information that pertains to a lot of job roles in order to recognise the observations when they present themselves. On the other hand you actually have to have this vast resource of data with which to pull from.

Any and every time I meet someone from a background or job role that I don't have a lot of information about I am immediately fascinated. It helps the development of my conversations with them but I must admit, this is for entirely self-serving reasons. I wish to learn more so I am able to see more of the world that is being shown to me. Here, I lay before you 2 stories of very different applications of this specific branch of deductive work from my experience over the same weekend on a course in London. The first was a pre-course event where the patrons would get together at a bar to hang out with the person who was leading the event. I was introduced to a number of people in an extremely humbling way. To this day, I still don't know how to properly take a compliment but that is by the by.

I was introduced to a lovely American lady as 'The Sherlock Guy' and she asked about the straw in my drink. At the time I had no idea about the reasons behind the change to paper straws, merely that there had been this change. I was complaining about its structural defects in the drink I was trying in vain to suck up. She spoke quite sincerely and with some degree of passion about the micro plastics concern within the oceans at the time. You could tell that this was something that meant a great deal to her. The night continued on and at a time when I was sat at a table with a Frenchman, and an Australian (I am removing everyone's name on the off chance they would have some concern with the retelling of the tale) about the possibilities of our memories when the micro plastics lady came to me to ask a question:

'So you could tell what someone does just by looking at them?'

A very particular and direct question which as I abducted, meant that she had been told about what I do and that she directed this towards a job role. Meaning that she either had an interest in the notion of reading people or she had a particularly interesting or niche job herself. As we spoke I noted that she is someone for whom being told they are beautiful was a regular occurrence and she was objectively a beautiful woman, her focus was actively not on this, she clearly liked to take care of herself both visually, physically and mentally. I had deduced that she was a cross fitter and as we were talking about the reason for her choosing Ugg boots, the conversation was changed by someone else and we never got back to it. I was thinking that she was a model of some sort. Not as a cheesy chat up line but she was a standout beautiful woman dressed for comfort. So someone who is aware of their looks to the point where they actively don't want to focus on this and would prioritise comfort when all others and indeed the situation dictate some kind of a requirement for preening would indicate that she spends a great deal of time feeling uncomfortable in relation to looks. As such, a model would fit the description of all of those observations.

Turn to the next day after completing day 1. All of the patrons had gone out for a meal and a few drinks as organised by the course leader and I had joined a conversation where the 'model' lady in question was talking about her experiences of training privately on a 1on1 basis with the course leader as a testament of sorts to the skills that she was learning. She had mentioned that she had gone to an event of sorts with him as a way to put her skills to a practical test. She told this story of how she turned a conversation around because this 'bitch turned cold when I told her what I do for a living' and a few sentences later she muttered off hand 'that's usually the case when people find out what I do'. Now that would invite questions around the topic of what she does for a living right? However this was clearly something the model was used to navigating as she moved the story right along to what she did in order to turn this around.

That right there is all you need. All you need to develop something in order to infer what someone does for a living. Look at everything I had gathered up until that moment:

- Environmentally conscious
- Ecologically conscious
- Aware of her looks
- Preference for taking care of herself in all forms
- Job is a taboo of sorts. Enough that she would bring it up initially and enough that it could turn a bitch cold. As it does normally to women.

A socially polarising job that takes into account that of her looks. It was very likely that she wasn't a beauty pageant winner at the local KKK meetings. So I arrived at 'works in the adult industry' in some form. A glamour model or something like that. I didn't pursue it any further because though she was initially curious as to me being able to see this, it was clearly quite a sore subject for her so I let it be and thought nothing of it. The final day of the course arrived and the course leader had mentioned a celebrity in our midst. I began looking around in vain for an actor or singer. That's usually who people mean when they say celebrity. He then, stifling a playful chuckle might I add, stated that we have the 'Second highest rated pornstar in the world on the course'. I instantly knew who he meant. It was the model. I wish I could have chatted to her more in order to learn about the role as I genuinely have questions that I feel would have helped me to spot that sooner. Despite what some of you sordid folks may be thinking at the moment, I would have asked the same questions of a male as I would a female.

A missed opportunity to learn from someone who works in an area of the world that is a multi-billion dollar industry, and yet you don't ordinarily bump into Adult entertainers in the pub down the road. Anyway, moving on to the other tale and yet we stay on the end of day 1 meal from the same course. It turns out that they were all pretty familiar with The Monographs which was both a lovely experience and unnerving at times as being on a course I was engaged in full 'work mode' not 'talk mode'. I was talking to a group of guys about deduction and its processes. There was a French guy in the group, an Australian, 2 Englishmen, an American and a Brazilian. I noticed the Brazilian guy smiling with intrigue. I knew a question or challenge of some sort was on the way. The smile is often confused with ego but it is not the case in this situation. It is more disbelief and genuine curiosity. It is more as if someone is smiling to say, 'Nah that can't be real but I really hope it is.' He was waiting for his moment that eventually came and he said, 'Go on then, what do I do for a living?'

Now bear in mind that at no point throughout the entire course had anyone mentioned this deductive feat. I cite these two stories so that you will be aware of just how often I am asked about this in isolated moments. You never want to miss an opportunity to practise after all.

He was, to use the modern parlance, a short king, wearing jeans, a fitted shirt that was loosely tucked in, a blazer and his hair was gelled nicely and styled with his hands. He smelled good as well. The aftershave was nice though I didn't recognise the brand. His shoes though! His beautifully demonstrative shoes were the key! They were brown leather and came to a point at the front. Either well maintained, new or both. Let's sum this up again:

- Aware of the perceived need to dress smartly for social occasions even though it was never stated as anything resembling a requirement
- Confident, inquisitive, zealous, well spoken, clean
- Shoes built for style more so than comfort of any sort. Toes aren't meant to be in the position that they have to be in for those shoes.

All of this put together to make what I felt to be the dictionary definition of a salesman. I sent this assessment back towards him after a few seconds. He confidently responded ,"No, not really." Always keen to learn from my mistakes I asked him ."Oh cool, so what do you do for a living then?" His answer still has me curious to this day. Now just to qualify this, time has no doubt affected the exact wording of what he said but it was because I was so baffled by the information that I didn't remember it word for word. His answer was words to the effect of:

Brazilian ,"I actually work with a partner and I go to businesses to tell them about the courses that we run and then my partner goes to teach them once I have the contracts signed."

After a few stunned beats I said:

Ben ,"So, you're a salesman then?"

Needless to say he accepted my assessment when everyone else pointed out to him as well that what he was saying was in fact someone involved in the selling of things. So what then, I hear you cry, is the point of me telling you all of this? It is to simply say, that 'the rules' for being able to deduce what someone does for a living, don't exist.

To suggest that they exist would be to intimate that you can solve the unsolvable as you would need to move with times, culture, fashion, job roles and a myriad of other things. Being able to notice what someone does for a living could be the most absurdly simple observation you will ever make. When standing in the middle of a shopping centre area and someone walks past you wearing the black and white smile of the infamous colonel then you would know they work for KFC. If you saw someone wearing green khaki style trousers and steel toe capped boots with a pair of transparent rubber gloves hanging out of their pockets you would know that they very likely worked on an ambulance in some capacity. If you heard someone talk about the issues with Iambic pentameter in the 3rd stanza then you would know they teach English in some form. I mean the list really could go on and on. It would all come back to the back of knowledge you are looking to develop or whether or not you are looking for shortcuts. Not in a bitchy high and mighty sense but merely in an attempt to help you see past the romanticising of the task itself.

Once these rose tinted glasses fall off you will be able to see the information that is right in front of you and how it might relate to the task at hand. If you are looking for jobs specifically it will blind you to the other information that may end up being more relevant and get in the way of your curiosity. Here is a list of some of the misses that have occurred and what my curiosity led to as a result.

- The first time I met a sous chef I had managed to figure out that she worked in hospitality in some form but no further. I then spent the next 30 minutes talking to her about the best practices in the kitchen for work with knives.
- The first time I met a stripper was at a friend's Bachelor party and I spent 45 minutes talking to her about the specific shoe requirements she had for whether or not she was working a pole.
- The first time I met a Lighting Technician we spent time talking about the specific marks on his hands and more specifically how naturally strong his handshake was even though he seemed to think he was not strong at all.
- The first time I met a bookstore owner we spoke more about the psychology of not getting high on your own supply. As in, spending more time reading than working.

Had I spent time actively looking for something that connected to a bookstore owner for example, they would have had to have been wearing a Librarian costume and instead I walked away with more valuable information for my memory palace each time. Final thoughts then 'Stay Curious.'

The Hounds

'Dogs don't make mistakes.' Sherlock Holmes - Silver Blaze

The work in this chapter may rival my fondness for the information connected to tattoos. Not just because I am heavily tattooed and prefer talking to dogs than I do most people. It is because this is a treasure trove of data that is on the surface, indirect in its observation but offers direct and personal insight into someone else's life. How they care for an animal of any sort is very telling indeed. The talk of objects being outwardly reflective of someone's life has gone on for some time but there is (to my mind) nothing quite like the active lovable animal that lives with any of the people in question. That is not to say non-domesticated animals aren't just as fun to read, it is just that they aren't very common at all.

I owe a huge amount of work in this area to Sam Gosling, so I would encourage all of you to read everything that you can from him on this topic. It does seem a little in poor taste to reduce the insights into a life with animals to a list of applicable heuristics and yet, here we are. It is much the same as reducing the insights into a piece of complex machinery to a few points and yet we can do the same. You will find a little cross over with some of the beginning points. With so many things on the plant for us to work with, the requirement for us having a similar starting area to begin our observation journey would only make sense.

Requirements

Each animal has its own sub set of requirements for care. There are a certain list of things that you have to do to take care of a dog, just as there are for a Horse. These details would be worlds apart and yet the mechanics of starting remain the same. What do you need to get and what do you need to do in order to properly take care of the animal in question? This is not a subjective response but the acknowledgement of the requirements for the animal to flourish in your care. These are unavoidable as you would be taking care of an animal that doesn't think of the world in anywhere close to the same way as you do.

So this would present a kind of tick box list for you to go through:
- Well fed
- Clean
- Healthy
- Regular exercise
- Mood regulators and behavioural care
- Interaction and play

Now there are a few more specifics when you look towards some of the more niche animals that can be cared for. However, if you stick to the above headings, you will go a long, long way.

A Gigantic Hound

Being the dog lover that I am, I can use our old friends the canines to illustrate this breakdown for you. However, this will all depend on the presentation of the information you are seeing. It is not every day that you will see exactly what each animal is fed. This will be in very specific circumstances. So it is best to prepare you for all that you may stand a chance of seeing.

The food is something that many tend to argue over given that there are so many varieties of everything and each with its own unique selling point. So in times like this I have a way in which I like to operate. I am aware that most people seem to be familiar with the missing number maths puzzles like something from a Fibonacci sequence. They tend to look like this:

3, 5, 8, 13, 21, 34, 55, 89

Your task would then be to figure out what the next number in the sequence would be. Now there are much more mathematically sound ways to approach this but I use these as an allegory for problem solving when I am seemingly overwhelmed with information to see and sift through. You could look at the initial list of numbers and then go a step lower to find out what the correlations between each would be. In the above case, the sequence that exists between would be:
2, 3, 5, 8, 13, 21, 34

You could do this again and again if you need to in order to better understand the presentation of the initial pattern. In this case it is the standard Fibonacci sequence where you add the previous 2 numbers together to give you the next. 2+3 gives you 5. 5+3 gives you 8. 8+5 gives you 13 and so on. When you reduce it down far enough you can find a workable pattern in order to figure out information from the original sequence. We reduce the requirements for food down to its base and it comes back to cost. Not a rant about the consumer models for business but simply that the cost of something is how we can split the difference on someone's motivation for its purchase. This in turn gives you direct information about the owner.

Option one for memory palace development presents itself. What is it that makes pet food good for you? Here are some key components that should be included in high-quality dog food:

- Protein: Dogs are carnivores, so a good dog food should have a high-quality source of animal protein, such as chicken, beef, or fish.
- Carbohydrates: Dogs need carbohydrates for energy, and a good dog food should include easily digestible sources like whole grains or vegetables.
- Fats: Healthy fats, such as omega-3 and omega-6 fatty acids, contribute to a shiny coat, healthy skin, and overall vitality.
- Vitamins and Minerals: Essential vitamins and minerals, like vitamin A, vitamin D, calcium, and phosphorus, are

necessary for your dog's overall health, growth, and development.

- Fibre: Adequate fibre content helps with digestion and maintains a healthy digestive system.
- No artificial additives: Avoid dog foods with artificial colours, flavours, preservatives, or fillers.

Remember, every dog is unique, so it's important to consider your dog's specific needs, age, breed, and any dietary restrictions they may have when selecting the right dog food. Consulting with your veterinarian can help you make an informed decision. Before this turned into a PSA from me on dog food, this would offer you insight in terms of what it is that makes a pet food expensive or not. If it is that expensive pet food and the supermarket home brand does the same thing then why buy one over the other? This gets us to our motivations that surround the cost of an item.

We can learn so much about an individual based on how they choose to spend their disposable income. Imagine having a spare fiver in your pocket. What would you spend it on? This would be very revealing about your motivations in life. The same is said in this scenario. The general rule of thumb is that there are more of the proteins, carbs, fats, vitamins and minerals in the expensive food when compared to the cheaper items however, this is not true right the way across the board. So we can add into this further insight as to how much value someone has in their life for the 'finer things' as opposed to the things that actually matter.

This then presents a new piece of information that can be used. There are, at the time of writing, an estimated 250 different brands and varieties of dog food that can be purchased in the UK. We could go beneath the available data to try and understand which is considered more readily accessible than other brands in order to understand how detailed the owner(s) of their animals are. Though this is all specified in relation to dogs, the topics and insights remain the same for pretty much any domesticated animal other than the more exotic kinds. Though given their sparsity in terms of numbers, that is something I won't be going into in this book.

Clean and Healthy

I am putting these 2 together for now given how closely linked they are. Though cleanliness can be very situational unlike the health of the animals in question. When you think of a clean and healthy human, you think of them, objectively speaking of course, as well kept and body size in form with their frame. As in, it is quite easy to spot someone who is under or overweight and someone that doesn't wash themselves as often as they should. So what we are looking to do here is to qualify the cleanliness regime of the animal based on how long their fur is. Obviously the more they have, or the thicker it is or even both. The more challenging and targeted the cleaning of the animal needs to be.

You can spend some of your time looking into the diagnostics of canine or any domesticated animal if you choose. Though outside of a veterinary practice, this may be a waste of your time and effort. The humble Shih-tzu is the most common long haired dog in the UK at the time of writing. 8th on a global scale. When you look at a Shih Tzu you might immediately be drawn to a dirty face and think, dirty dog and therefore they belong to uncaring owners. This would be the flaw in your chain of reasoning from the get-go. When you are a long haired dog, anything and everything that comes near your face is going to leave a trace. Especially when it is food and drink. Imagine a human with a massive beard relative to the size of their face. So this would then indicate to you as the observer that you would need to not only take the creation of the dog itself, but also the health signs that may be indicated.

We can reduce this down into 2 characteristics for the everyday observer - Malnutrition and irregular moods. Signs of malnutrition in dogs can vary depending on the severity and duration of the condition. Here are some common signs to watch out for:

Weight Loss: Unexplained or rapid weight loss is a clear indicator of malnutrition. Dogs that are not receiving adequate nutrition will lose body fat and muscle mass.

Lethargy: Malnourished dogs often lack energy and appear lethargic. They may be less interested in play, exercise, or even basic activities.

Dull Coat and Skin Issues: A dog's coat may become dry, brittle, and lacklustre when they're not getting proper nutrition. Skin problems like flakiness, itching, and irritations can also be indications of malnutrition.

Loss of Appetite: While it might seem counterintuitive, malnourished dogs might lose their appetite as their bodies become weaker. They may be unable to maintain their normal eating habits.

Weakness and Muscle Atrophy: Malnutrition can lead to muscle weakness and even muscle wasting, where a dog's muscles visibly shrink.

Digestive Issues: Malnourished dogs can experience digestive problems like diarrhoea, vomiting, and constipation due to their weakened immune and digestive systems.

Behavioural Changes: Dogs that are malnourished might display changes in behaviour, becoming more irritable, anxious, or even aggressive.

Dental Problems: Poor nutrition can lead to dental issues, including gum disease and tooth decay.

Delayed Healing: Wounds and injuries may take longer to heal in malnourished dogs due to a compromised immune system.

Stunted Growth (in Puppies): Puppies that do not receive proper nutrition may experience stunted growth and fail to reach their expected size and development milestones.

Behavioural changes in dogs can be indicative of various underlying issues, so it's important to consider the context and any potential triggers. Here are some significant signs of behavioural changes in dogs:

Aggression: Sudden aggression, whether directed towards people, other animals, or objects, is a notable behaviour change that could signal fear, pain, or a territorial issue.

Excessive Barking: If a dog starts barking excessively or more than usual, it could be a sign of anxiety, boredom, or a response to something in their environment.

Sudden Fear or Anxiety: If a dog becomes fearful, anxious, or nervous in situations where they were previously confident, it might indicate an underlying stressor.

Destructive Behaviour: Increased destructive behaviour, such as chewing on furniture or other objects, can suggest boredom, anxiety, or separation distress.

Changes in Appetite: A sudden loss of appetite or increased appetite could be linked to medical issues or emotional stress.

Excessive Licking or Scratching: Dogs that constantly lick, chew, or scratch themselves might be experiencing discomfort, allergies, or skin issues.

Isolation or Clinginess: If a social dog becomes overly clingy or avoids interaction, it could signal physical discomfort or emotional distress.

Sudden House Training Problems: Dogs that were previously housetrained but start having accidents might have medical problems or stress-related issues.

Changes in Sleep Patterns: A dog that starts sleeping excessively or having trouble sleeping might be facing physical discomfort or anxiety.

Avoidance Behaviour: Dogs that suddenly avoid specific places, people, or situations they used to be comfortable with could be responding to negative associations.

Excessive Panting or Pacing: These behaviours might indicate pain, anxiety, or restlessness.

Changes in Playfulness: A formerly playful dog that becomes disinterested in toys or play sessions could be feeling unwell or experiencing a shift in mood.

Excessive Salivation: Dogs that start drooling excessively might be stressed or experiencing nausea.

Tail Position: A dog that holds its tail in a different position (tucked between legs, raised more than usual) might be trying to communicate discomfort or fear.

Changes in Grooming Habits: A decrease in grooming or excessive grooming might signal stress or physical issues.

When you observe significant behavioural changes in your dog, it's essential to consider recent events, changes in routine, and any potential health issues. If the behaviour change is sudden, severe, or persistent, consulting with a veterinarian or a professional dog behaviourist is recommended to address the underlying cause and determine the best course of action.

When a dog is getting plenty of exercise, interaction, and play, their overall demeanour and behaviour will reflect a balanced and fulfilled lifestyle. Here are some signs that indicate a dog is receiving adequate physical activity, social interaction, and playtime:

Happy Demeanour: The dog appears generally happy, content, and excited about life.

Energetic and Playful: The dog eagerly engages in play, displaying enthusiasm and energy during activities.

Relaxed Behaviour: When not playing, the dog is calm and relaxed, often enjoying downtime without signs of restlessness.

Good Appetite: Dogs that are well-exercised tend to have a healthy appetite and eat regularly.

Healthy Weight: The dog maintains a healthy body weight without being overweight or underweight.

Responsive to Commands: A dog that's regularly exercised and engaged is more likely to respond well to training commands.

Proper Sleep Patterns: Adequately exercised dogs typically sleep well at night and may take regular naps during the day.

Play Initiations: The dog initiates play with toys, other dogs, or even humans, showing a desire for interaction.

Calm Greetings: Dogs that are well-exercised are more likely to greet people calmly, without excessive jumping or hyperactivity.

Improved Behaviour: Regular exercise and playtime can reduce behaviours like excessive barking, digging, and chewing on inappropriate objects.

Strong Bonds: Dogs that interact with their owners and other dogs regularly tend to develop strong social bonds and better interpersonal skills.

Explorative Behaviour: A well-exercised dog may show curiosity and interest in exploring new environments and smells.

Satisfactory Body Condition: The dog's body condition score is appropriate – they're not overly skinny or excessively obese.

Tolerant of Alone Time: Dogs that receive sufficient mental and physical stimulation are often more comfortable being alone for reasonable periods.

Engagement with Enrichment Toys: Dogs that enjoy puzzles, interactive toys, and mental challenges demonstrate an engaged and active mind.

Tail Wagging: A dog that's happy and fulfilled will often have a loose and wagging tail.

Positive Social Interactions: Dogs that interact well with other dogs and people are likely to have a balanced social life.

Variety in Play: Engaged dogs tend to enjoy a variety of play activities, such as fetching, tug-of-war, and chasing games.

Remember that different breeds and individual dogs have varying exercise and interaction needs, so it's important to note that the aforementioned points, as well as everything else prior to that, are the corollaries across pretty much every breed.

Features of the Animal's Life

When you bring an animal into your life, in whatever kind of domesticated sort your local area allows, there are a certain number of things you will need in order to make sure the animal can exist. To say this out loud seems almost too obvious and yet these are the factors that will very often go under the radar as being suggestive of information for the simple fact that they are so common. It is with that in mind that the following paragraphs exist and yet I will do my best to keep this as short as possible.

Owning a cat requires what elements at a very basic level? Bowls for food, the food itself, toys, litter tray and maybe a travel crate at most right? From here the variations will be more suggestive of the animals presence in the owners life. So when you think of food bowls, what do you think of? There are degrees to even this. If you were to buy something of the everyday variety like a pen or a bottle of water for example. There are versions of these that might cost £1 at the most

and there are some versions that might cost £5 at a minimum. What would be the difference in those things really when you think about them? Not a lot really. So when you look at the cat bowls that are displayed in the picture through this link, there is a world of difference between them. I tell you that one of them cost £2 and the other cost £17, which way around would you say that would go? We are now back into the realm of money that I really love, in terms of valuable insight. Why would someone choose to spend £15 more on something that does the same thing? The answer to that question will give you a fair number of observations to explore with regards to this. Here is another question that will very often not be thought about. How many different kinds of dog leads are there?

At the time of writing there are several different types of dog leads/leashes available, each designed to serve specific purposes and meet various needs. Here are some of the most common types of dog leads:

Standard Leash: This is the most common type of leash, typically made of nylon or leather, with a handle on one end and a clip to attach to the dog's collar or harness on the other end.

Retractable Leash: These leashes have a retractable cord or tape that allows the dog to roam more freely while still being under control. They often come with a locking mechanism to control the length of the leash.
Adjustable Leash: These leashes can be adjusted to different lengths, allowing you to have more control in different situations.

Training Lead: Also known as a long line, this type of lead is longer than a standard leash and is often used for training purposes, giving the dog more freedom while still maintaining control.

Slip Lead: A slip lead combines a collar and leash in one piece. It tightens around the dog's neck when pulled, which can be useful for training or quick control.

Martingale Lead: This is a combination of a collar and a limited-slip leash, designed to prevent dogs from slipping out of the collar. It tightens slightly when the dog pulls, providing more control.

Harness Lead: This type of leash attaches to a harness rather than a collar. It can help distribute pressure more evenly and is often used for dogs that pull a lot.

Hands-Free Leash: These leashes are designed to be worn around the owner's waist or across the body, allowing them to walk or run with their hands free.

Two-Dog Leash: These leashes are designed to walk two dogs simultaneously on a single lead.

Bungee Leash: This type of leash has a built-in bungee-like section that absorbs shock when the dog pulls, making walks more comfortable for both the dog and the handler.

Seat Belt Leash: These leashes are designed to attach to your dog's harness and then clip into a seatbelt slot, securing your dog while driving.

Reflective Leash: These leashes have reflective materials woven into the fabric, making them more visible in low light conditions.

Chain Leash: A chain leash is often made of metal and can be useful for dogs that tend to chew on their leash.

Multi-Function Leash: Some leashes are designed with multiple functions, such as converting from a regular leash to a hands-free leash or a double dog leash.

The choice for the owners depends on the dog's size, behaviour, and specific needs during walks or other activities. A general rule of thumb would be that the thicker the rope/cord/metal the leash is made from, the bigger the dog will be. Each one of these elements, once observed, provide a significant insight into an owner's life with their animal. Now I could spend the next few pages going into the ways this would be relevant to each and every domesticated animal in the world; however, I am a firm believer that this kind of background knowledge is something that you can build up over life or when you have time. It shouldn't be a primary function of your reading in the early stages.

Personal-ity

"Tell me what you own, and I will tell you who you are." - André Maurois

There was as much of a challenge writing this chapter as there was writing it the first time around. The balance needs to be struck between it being not just a list of items and the information that is attached which could potentially go on forever and something that is going to be enjoyable to read. So let's cover the sub field of psychological research known as Material Possessions and Identity.

Material Possessions and Identity focuses on understanding how an individual's possessions, belongings, and the way they interact with their environment can provide insights into their identity, personality, values, emotions, and well-being. It's an area of research that explores the relationship between material possessions and the way people construct and express their sense of self.

There are several key concepts and principles that comprise this area:

Symbolic Meaning: Material possessions are often more than just physical objects – they carry symbolic meaning and can represent various aspects of an individual's life. For example, a person's choice of clothing, decorations, or personal items can reflect their cultural background, hobbies, memories, and personal beliefs.

In the contemporary landscape of 2023, the concept of material possessions carrying symbolic meaning has taken on new dimensions and relevance. The items people choose to own and display have become powerful channels for self-expression, mirroring the complex tapestry of their identities and engaging with the evolving socio-cultural environment. I would qualify someone's social media channels within this arena as well given the type of content they put out and/or interact with.

In this era, the role of material possessions as virtual conduits of symbolic significance has expanded to encompass a wide range of items, both physical and digital. Clothing choices have become even more pronounced as reflections of individuality. Look at the ways in which the simple jeans with holes in them are lambasted by some and heralded as stunning by others even though in some cases the entire front part of the leg is missing. Styles, patterns, and fashion brands selected by individuals are no longer just about personal taste; they often communicate affiliations with social movements, advocate for sustainable practices, or embrace cultural diversity. The very act of wearing a certain type of clothing has evolved into a statement that signifies alignment with specific values and ideologies.

Decorative items, particularly those found in living spaces and digital environments, have gained heightened importance in conveying not only personal aesthetics but also narratives of identity. Home decor choices now encompass pieces that reflect an individual's commitment to eco-consciousness or innovation. Minimalist designs signal a desire for simplicity and detachment from consumerism, while maximalist displays celebrate a love for vibrant cultures and experiences. In the digital realm, virtual home environments in social media platforms and virtual reality spaces have also emerged as extensions of one's identity, further emphasising the linkage between possessions and self-expression. Everything from Cheetos and Greggs to BLM and feminism have their own clothing line for example. Very different affinities that are symbolised through the same mode, clothing.

Personal items have similarly evolved to hold more profound meaning in 2023. Gadgets and technology have become integral to daily life, transcending their functional roles. The type of smartphone, wearable tech, or electronic devices a person carries now reflects their tech-savviness, connection to the digital world, and alignment with ethical tech consumption. Personal mementos like photographs have also transformed as they migrate to digital formats, but their preservation signifies the continuity of cherished memories and the fusion of past and present.

The prevalence of social and political activism in contemporary society has imbued material possessions with the power to advocate for change. Accessories adorned with symbols of unity, justice, and equality enable individuals to broadcast their support for various causes. Ownership of sustainable products and ethically sourced materials functions as a testament to a commitment to environmental well-being. You will see this in everything from bangles and bracelets to earrings and pin badges.

In the dynamic milieu of 2023, material possessions stand as more than passive artefacts; they serve as potent agents of communication, narrative-building, and cultural participation. With the expansion of digital presence and the convergence of personal and public spheres, the symbolic meanings embedded within possessions have gained an amplified voice, allowing individuals to articulate their beliefs, values, and aspirations in ever more intricate and interconnected ways.

Self-Expression: People use their possessions as a means of self-expression. The objects they own can communicate to others who they are, what they value, and what they aspire to be. This form of self-presentation allows individuals to shape how they are perceived by others. The intricate interplay between material possessions and self-expression has taken on new dimensions, spurred on by the integration of digital platforms, evolving fashion trends, and heightened social consciousness. Material possessions today extend beyond their physical form, becoming digital representations and emblems of identity in an interconnected world.

In this era, self-expression through possessions encompasses not only physical items but also extends to the virtual realm. A realm that at the time of writing, I am only slightly getting used to. The digital age has given rise to a new form of ownership – the possession of digital assets and virtual items. From coveted skins and accessories in online gaming to customised avatars and virtual environments in augmented reality, individuals are using these digital possessions to project facets of their identity and affiliations within online communities. The symbolic value of digital items is further heightened by the rise of non-fungible tokens (NFTs), which authenticate ownership of unique digital assets, reinforcing the perception of digital items as authentic expressions of identity.

The prevalence of social media platforms has turned personal belongings into carefully curated stages for self-presentation. Fashion choices are meticulously assembled not only to reflect individual aesthetics but to communicate social and cultural allegiances. Clothing bearing social justice slogans, sustainable fashion brands, or symbols of specific causes exemplify the fusion of self-expression with broader social discourse. Moreover, the selfie culture has turned accessories like smartphone cases, camera gear, and even the choice of photo backgrounds into key components of self-expression, offering glimpses into personal interests and creative inclinations.

The concept of self-expression through material possessions has transcended traditional boundaries, incorporating digital possessions and leveraging online platforms to amplify personal narratives. As individuals continue to navigate the virtual and physical realms, their material and digital possessions stand as vibrant canvases for communicating who they are, what they stand for, and the communities they belong to. The amalgamation of physical and virtual belongings in the sphere of self-expression reaffirms the notion that possessions are not just objects but dynamic extensions of identity, weaving intricate stories in a world increasingly characterised by fluidity and connectivity.

Identity Formation: The possessions a person selects and surrounds themselves with play a role in shaping their identity. They help individuals create a sense of continuity and coherence in their life story. The profound role of material possessions in shaping identity has evolved to incorporate a diverse array of items that span physical, virtual, and hybrid dimensions. Possessions have become integral tools in crafting and narrating one's identity, reflecting the multifaceted nature of modern life and the intricate interplay between the tangible and the intangible. It has almost become cliche to know that someone's online presence is different to how they are in real life. I mean look at the way that 'Influencers' take photographs of their favourite tea through their cleavage or pointing towards the best protein to take through a clenched bicep.

The prevalence of subscription-based services and the sharing economy has introduced a new layer to identity formation through possessions. Ownership is no longer the sole marker of identity; access to experiences, memberships, and digital subscriptions contributes to one's sense of self. Streaming platforms, wellness apps, and co-working space memberships become badges of identity, reflecting personal interests, values, and aspirations. The curation of these intangible possessions showcases a contemporary approach to identity, where choices are not confined to physical accumulation but encompass the cultivation of meaningful experiences and connections.

The process of identity formation through material possessions has transitioned into an expansive and interconnected endeavour. The fusion of physical and digital realms, the emergence of subscription-based identities, and the cultivation of experiences have collectively reshaped the way individuals engage with their possessions. As people curate their environments and choose their possessions, they are not only assembling collections of items but intricately weaving a tapestry that communicates their past, present, and envisioned future. In this era of limitless possibilities, material possessions stand as tangible chapters in the ongoing narrative of identity, revealing the rich complexities that shape individuals in an ever-evolving world.

The following points would be other aspects that would require consideration in your reading of the objects in your surroundings:

- **Attachment and Emotional Significance**: Material possessions can hold emotional significance, serving as reminders of meaningful experiences, relationships, or life milestones. They can provide comfort and a sense of security.
- **Consumption Patterns**: The way individuals acquire, use, and discard possessions can reveal patterns of consumption and lifestyle choices. For instance, a minimalist lifestyle versus a tendency to accumulate possessions can reflect different attitudes toward materialism.
- **Psychological Well-Being**: Researchers in this field explore how possessions contribute to an individual's psychological well-being. For some people, certain possessions may act as

sources of stress, while for others, they may offer comfort and satisfaction.

Research Methods and Applications:

Researchers in the subfield of Material Possessions and Identity use various research methods to gain insights, including observation, surveys and interviews and content analysis.

There are applications of the research that we can look to consider moving forwards:

- Consumer Behaviour: Insights from this field can inform marketing strategies and product design by understanding the deeper motivations behind purchasing decisions.
- Therapeutic Interventions: Therapists can use discussions about material possessions to explore clients' self-identity, attachments, and emotional well-being.
- Environmental Psychology: This research can contribute to understanding the relationships between individuals, their possessions, and the environment, which can inform urban planning and design.

In essence, Material Possessions and Identity research seeks to uncover the intricate connections between the objects people own, the stories they tell, and the identities they construct. It sheds light on the ways in which individuals use material possessions to communicate their uniqueness and navigate the complexities of their lives. So rather than go into this phone and what it means in this context or this handbag and another context, I thought it best to equip you with a governing set of heuristics that you can use to tackle all items.

A Study in an example

The following will be details about an item that one of my friends has in their possession. I will specifically build this out in a step by step way to show additional contextual points and how this can change the information that connects to the person in question. I would like you to try and build this out following the questions I ask you along the way. Please, I implore you, play along with this and explore the observations you make. If you choose not to engage in these applications then this book will remain as something interesting you read one time. Totally within your rights but, the applications can start here. The growth can start now! Anyway, I'll climb down off my little soap box now and just get on with it.

There is a Samsung Galaxy S23 that has a Spigen Tough Armour case on. If you don't know what that is I would recommend that you google it now, otherwise this will make the next part very difficult. Now, I am going to presume you have googled this and are aware of its specificities. From here, grab an additional sheet of paper and begin the journey of exploring these points in line with everything we have covered in this book so far.

1. Why might someone choose that phone?
2. Why might someone choose that case?
3. What needs do the answers to the above questions fulfil?
4. What price range does that suggest?
5. What socio-economic background does that connect to?

It is important to stress at this stage that there will very likely be a number of answers to the above questions and that is perfectly fine. Even more so, that may be the best position to be in given the very limited insight I have given to you at the moment. The point is to go far beyond even these suggested questions to see what, if anything, this information could connect to.

Here is your next point of interest:

- The phone has a cracked screen protector

We begin again. What new questions does this present to you? How does it change the answers that you came up with to the original questions and the subsequent information that you built up the first time around. This continual evaluation of the additional data you are ingesting will constantly keep your end hypothesis in a continual state of flux and movement with the potential for change.

Here is the next point. Obtained after the phone is unlocked and its contents are now viewable:

- These are the most frequently used emoji's when sending messages

You know what to do by now. Re-evaluate, add on, manipulate, create alternatives. The point here is that you will never, I imagine as the odds would be astronomically against you, meet this person. So what you are doing here is developing a list of observations that you can use that would better inform your interactions with said individual.

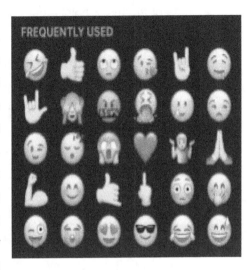

Final point I am going to give you:

- The open apps are, and in no particular order: Capcut, facebook, YouTube, WhatsApp, Instagram and Centr

For the final time, complete the process. At the end of this you will have a list of observations. Some that are very strong and are supported in other areas by other things and some that are not. This would be in reference to the size of the cluster you have been able to develop. You can then proceed with your strongest and most significant inferences to be able to break down the information that is connected to the owner of this phone.

Some of the major points that I deduce will have come out of this will be clumsiness, age, job/hobbies so I will confirm the basics for you and the rest is something that you could use should you ever interact with this person. As a cheeky ploy, if you follow along with my podcast *The Deductionist Podcast* in the near future then I will break down in full detail who this is.

Basics of who owns the phone:
- Male
- 32 years old
- Full time work - Delivery driver
- Not at all clumsy, just does his best to make sure his possessions are looked after
- Doesn't like his job and ideally would like to move into where his passions lie

You should, I hope, have built a lot more on the back of this. This information should not bias any potential interactions you have with this person. It should give you something to work with that when new information is presented to you, you will have the ability and the capacity to reformulate as needed. To be the alchemist of the information you observe in a way.

To conclude this may feel like an open ended response given the varying degrees of request for 'How to read.....' and then insert whatever name of the item is after the fact. The suspected guiding light being that there is some particular system for the understanding of the information that is connected to every single item that could ever exist. Given that you know how brains work, you know that doing things in this way simply isn't conducive to an effective way of utilising this information in the moment. Unless of course you have Hyperthymesia. In which case, I am so incredibly jealous of you right now!

You would be best served in using the above information to guide how you look at all items. You could get quite far on thinking about whether the item in question is expensive or not? What is its purpose? Is it taken care of? This alone would give you a lot of information to connect to its place in someone's life.

The Game is A-nother Foot

"The eyes can mislead, a smile can lie, but the shoes always tell the truth" - Gregory House

These are by far and away one of my favourite things to be asked to read information in. The reason is 2 fold. The first being that is never the way it appears on TV and it has become a small joyous experience in my life to burst the bubble of the way people are observed in reality when compared to the TV. So in essence this chapter could be built within the previous one. However there are a few singular things that are worth mentioning by themselves so, it has its own.

Here is the summation of my journey in discovering a governing set of ideas for us to work with. It is important to note that the reliable studies and figures that these are based on have stronger connections to market research than actual psychological studies. The ones that I have found over the years tend to have a very small sampling of a closed population by which they have developed their outcomes from. It does not mean that it is not valuable; after all for a market to succeed and bring in money then the information they use to base this on has to be sound.

Here are the foundational points of interest:

Physical Clues and Symbols: They can provide clues about their lifestyle, preferences, and sometimes even their profession. For example, the type of shoes someone wears might reflect their fashion taste, occupation (e.g., formal shoes for an office job, sneakers for a fitness trainer), or cultural background.

Status and Identity: Shoes and clothing can also be markers of social status, identity, and group affiliation. Certain brands, styles, or designs may carry symbolic meanings or indicate membership in a specific community or subculture.

Self-Presentation: People often make conscious choices about their appearance, including their footwear, as a form of self-presentation. By observing their choices, you might gain insight into how they want to be perceived by others.

Nonverbal Communication: Clothing and accessories, including shoes, can sometimes communicate nonverbal messages. Someone might choose to wear something that reflects their mood, personality, or a statement they want to make.

Cultural Significance: In some cultures, footwear holds cultural or traditional significance. By paying attention to the shoes someone wears, you might learn something about their cultural background or heritage.

Interpretation: However, it's important to remember that drawing conclusions solely based on someone's shoes can be risky. While you might gather some insights, it's not always accurate to judge

147

someone's personality, emotions, or experiences solely based on their footwear.

It's worth noting that the practice of reading someone "in their shoes" (in the literal sense) isn't a scientifically rigorous method for understanding someone's thoughts, feelings, or experiences. While it might provide some limited insights, it's infinitely better to engage in open communication and empathetic listening if you're seeking a deeper understanding of another person. From this, there are a series of questions that you can look to address any shoe you see and get your abductive and inductive reasoning on!

- **What is the shoe?** A simple and direct question. What is it? Is it a shined black leather set of brogues? A pair of flame ridden New Rocks? Or even a pair of 6 inch stilettos. The questions and points of inquiry give rise to your exploration of the shoe's purpose. These can also not forget price, size and likely location of purchase.

- **What is it made to do?** A question that extends the purpose of the shoe. So when you look at a pair of shined leather brogues, what are they made to do? What are a pair of brogues made in order for the owner to signify? Whether you work for a company that makes brogues or not, the answers that you develop to this question will revolve around the same premise - Status! Dare I say, even a knock off?

- **What foot can fit in there?** Literally a wide foot? Or a thin foot? A builder's foot? Margot Robbie's foot? (I am given to understand from the Barbie Trailer that she has an important one?) You will be looking at the shape of the shoe and whether or not it has buckled and/or been bent out of shape. A stiletto is made for a narrow foot. Therefore if you find a stiletto that is bent out of shape and has loose leather around the toes on a UK size 5, it will tell a very different story if this same stiletto is a UK size 10.

- **Can the foot move?** As in, does the shoe fit, and how well does it fit? The reason being is that I am looking to gain some kind of an assessment as to the prevalence of the shoe in the person's life. This will connect to whether or not it is their only shoes or if they have strong sentimental connections to them. I know from experience that this goes on. A few years ago my mum got me a custom pair of converse for Christmas, only they were close to 2 sizes too small. I still wore them as often as I could due to my dorky connections and the love that went into my mum deciding to do that for me. Even though at many a gig in London, my toes ended up bleeding.

- **What size are they?** This will give me a grounding in the overall size and weight distribution of the individual(s) I am observing. The proportion of foot size to height is by no means an exact science. There is natural variation in body proportions among individuals. However, there are general guidelines and methods to assess whether someone's feet might be considered too big or too small relative to their height. Shoe size is often used as a rough indicator of foot size. There are shoe size charts available that can give you an idea of what shoe size is typically associated with different foot lengths. However, keep in mind that shoe size can vary between brands and styles.

Proportions: One common guideline is that the length of a person's foot should be about 15-20% of their height. This means that if someone is 5 feet tall (60 inches), their foot length might fall in the range of about 9 to 12 inches. However, this is just a rough estimation and there can be exceptions.

Body Type: People with different body types might have different foot proportions. For instance, a taller person might have slightly larger feet compared to a shorter person, even if their proportions seem different.

Personal Variation: Genetics and ethnicity also play a role. People from different ethnic backgrounds might have different average foot sizes for a given height.

Comfort and Functionality: Ultimately, the most important factor is whether the person's feet are comfortable and functional for their daily activities. Feet that are too big or too small might pose comfort or health issues, so it's more crucial to focus on how the individual feels and whether they can move comfortably.

- **Are they marketed to a particular person or group?** I am basically running a social version of comparing and contrasting based on market trends and the culture of the society I am in at that particular time. In short, let's say I assess someone to be a Punk. Yet when I see them, they are wearing a pair of brown wingtips; they are very contrasting between the 2 groups. Brogues are not marketed towards punks. There is nothing to say that Brogues can't be bought by anyone for that matter, it is just that that is not who they are marketed towards. In this hypothetical punk having a pair, that would tell a very unique story that veers away from the traditional punk life.

Were you to look up the book The Meaning of Things: Domestic Symbols and the Self by Mihaly Csikszentmihalyi there are a number of takeaways that we can use that are particular to shoes. They stretch far beyond shoes as well but still, very applicable. The book introduces the concept of "object meanings," revealing that objects possess a layered significance beyond their tangible attributes. A shoe can serve a multifunctional purpose that is far beyond simply protecting our feet and style options. They can be demonstrative of wealth, interests and hobbies, tv or sports that you are a fan of, sociocultural background.

Look at the Vibram barefoot shoes. For those that don't know, these are the shoes with individual spaces for each of your toes. On the surface you could make the argument that, that is a needless flourish to a simple trainer that someone might use when going hiking. Yet if you look a little further in the kinesics behind them and the benefits towards movement and stability that we get out of using something like that, then owning them becomes something else altogether. Be careful that this does not lead you to reasoning information based on your own personal viewpoints of the item and ignoring the precise nature of what it is.

The book further highlights the interconnectedness of objects and the self, illustrating how the act of acquiring, arranging, and using possessions becomes a form of self-expression and identity validation. Furthermore, the authors explore the emotional ties individuals develop with their possessions, emphasising that these items often elicit sentimental attachments that bring comfort, nostalgia, or reassurance. We need look no further than the way shoes are arranged in the home. Though in some cases, not arranged in the home would be much more applicable. The arrangement of shoes on a shoe rack can provide a wide range of insights into a person's organisational tendencies, lifestyle preferences, and (no prizes for guessing why I like to see them) attention to detail. While it's important to note that these deductions can vary hugely depending on culture and building structure, here are some potential insights that can be gleaned from how someone arranges their shoes:

Orderliness and Organization: A neat and tidy arrangement of shoes suggests that the person values order and organisation. This would be demonstrated by however many pairs of shoes that are owned being together and facing the same way. They may have a methodical approach to their daily routines and enjoy maintaining a structured environment.

Priorities and Frequency of Use: The arrangement could reflect which shoes are worn most frequently. Shoes placed at the front or within easy reach might be the person's favourites or those they wear regularly, indicating their style preferences and comfort choices. The same could also be said of top shelf to bottom shelf. Think of convenience matched with a height assessment of the people in question.

Fashion Sense: The way shoes are organised can provide hints about the person's fashion preferences and awareness. If they have a variety of styles and brands neatly displayed, it could suggest an interest in fashion and keeping up with trends. Combine this observation with the priority insight for further support.

Personality Traits: A well-arranged shoe rack might indicate a person who is detail-oriented, conscientious, and likes to have things in their proper place. A more relaxed arrangement might suggest a more laid-back and spontaneous personality.

Attachment to Possessions: The condition of the shoes and how they're displayed can reveal how much the person values their belongings. Well-maintained shoes might indicate a strong sense of ownership and care for their possessions. Lower on the end of financial well-being leading to a need to prolong the life of the items they have could also play a part here.

Time Management: An organised arrangement can also imply that the person values efficiency and time management. They may prioritise finding their shoes quickly without unnecessary searching. So the opposite can also become relevant when shoes are strewn about the place with reckless abandon. Think of the average child and the parents' continuous complaint about putting their shoes away.

Space Management: How shoes are spaced on the rack could indicate how the person utilises their available space. An efficient use of space might suggest resourcefulness and the ability to maximise what they have. Racks that are hanging on the back of doors is always a good insight here.

Commitment to Maintenance: Shoes that are kept clean and polished might reflect the person's commitment to self-care and personal appearance. Clean and polished and on a rack is quite a feat of care given the nature of Locard's exchange principle.

Attachment to Sentimental Items: If there are shoes with sentimental value or ones that are rarely worn but kept for sentimental reasons, this might reveal an attachment to memories and emotions associated with objects. To decipher this as a possibility you would be looking for a distinct separation of the shoes from the bigger collections. In usual circumstances they would be kept in boxes and/or bags.

Variety of Activities: The types of shoes present and how they're organised could indicate the person's range of activities and hobbies. A mix of athletic shoes, casual shoes, and formal shoes might suggest a diverse lifestyle. A simple enough task to research the requirements in this area. Google 'What are the specific requirements for a basketball shoe' and then swap out the hobby as needed.

Remember that these interpretations can vary widely based on an individual's specific circumstances and personal habits. While the arrangement of shoes can offer insights, it's just one small piece of the puzzle when trying to understand someone's personality and lifestyle. This can very often be used as a springboard to other areas of the person's life. However it is worth noting that in order to view the shoes in the aforementioned manner it would require being able to review a cross section of what they own or listening to them being discussed. I shouldn't have to tell you at this stage that that represents a very specific situation indeed.

The Sign of Full - Bars

"A smartphone is a tool. A phone is a tool. They are both useful, but you have to use them with intention." - Elizabeth Dunn

What can be said about these things that has not been said already. They seem to be, as Homer might say of Alcohol 'The cause of and solution to, all of life's problems'. Given our global obsession with these things they have had such a predominant knock on effect in our lives that it is almost a certainty that someone who is of the age enough to have some kind of a conversation with, will have their phone on them at any time. It is something that I dabbled with as part of my act many moons ago when simulating some of the stunts from the Vaudevillian era. Knowing what someone has in their pockets and guessing someone's weight, that sort of thing. Which pocket in particular was the only challenge really, but it gave me something to work with, with anyone that came to the show.

Think about everything that we now run through our smart devices that are locked by only a 4-6 digit code, regardless of whether this is a drag and drop symbol or not. It holds your banking information and connected cards, your online activity, your social media activity, your private messages, your shopping, your photos, your modern life in short. To neglect the inferences that can be contained in a mobile phone, however smart it may be, is a fool's errand.

The branch of psychological research that delves into understanding people based on how they use their mobile phones is often referred to as (I shit you not) 'Mobile Phone Psychology'. How unimaginative is that title?! This area of research focuses on studying the behavioural, cognitive, emotional, and social aspects of individuals' interactions with their mobile devices.

Researchers in this field examine various aspects of mobile phone usage, such as:

Usage Patterns: Usage patterns in mobile phone usage analysis delve into the intricate details of how individuals interact with their devices on a daily basis. These patterns encompass the frequency, duration, and timing of mobile phone usage and serve as valuable insights into the routines and habits of users. The frequency of usage is an aspect of usage patterns that examines how often individuals engage with their mobile phones. It involves quantifying the number of times a user unlocks their phone, checks notifications, or launches applications throughout the day. Understanding frequency sheds light on the degree of dependence on the device and the role it plays in one's daily life. For example, frequent usage might indicate a heavy reliance on the phone for communication, work, or entertainment. The duration of usage is something beyond frequency, the duration of mobile phone usage provides a deeper perspective into how much time individuals spend on their devices during each interaction. Analysing the duration of app usage, screen time, or phone calls can reveal priorities and interests.

Extended periods of usage may suggest engagement in tasks like content consumption, gaming, or professional activities. The timing of usage examines when users are most active on their devices. This aspect considers daily routines, such as the hours of the day when individuals engage with their phones most frequently. It can highlight peak usage periods, such as early mornings, work hours, or late evenings, and offer insights into how mobile phones integrate into daily schedules.

Understanding these usage patterns goes beyond mere data collection; it enables researchers and analysts to draw meaningful conclusions about user behaviour. For instance, if a person consistently checks their email app first thing in the morning, it suggests a work-oriented routine. Conversely, frequent social media usage during lunch breaks may indicate a preference for connecting with friends and peers during leisure moments.

Businesses and app developers can leverage these insights to tailor their products and services to align with users' daily routines and habits. For researchers, it opens avenues to explore the relationship between mobile phone usage and various aspects of life, including productivity, mental well-being, and lifestyle choices. For us, there are several ways that we can get to grips with this kind of information within a few seconds. Though it would take into account the context in which you are using the phone and whether you have it locked or unlocked. We will look at passwords shortly.

Let us say in this first case, you have the phone unlocked and you need a quick assessment of the usage stats to further the profile you are developing of this hypothetical individual. Head to the settings in both Apple and Android models but for Apple you will need to search for Screen Time and in Android phones you will need to search for Digital Wellbeing and Parental Controls. Here you will get a breakdown of these usage statistics in an easily digestible manner. Top used apps, when they are used and for how long as well.

Invariably this is split between the particular day you are looking at and the total of the weeks' worth of information up until that stage. So if you are reviewing this on a Monday then this will be the same outcome.

Daily averages are split between the most used apps and the most notifications that are received to that particular app. 40-50 notifications through Signal on a Friday and excessive use of zoom and the mail service over Friday and into the weekend tells a very different story to someone whose usage shows 30-45 notifications through Snapchat and top used apps are TikTok, Instagram, facebook and snapchat where they notch up 4-5 hours a day over each of them.

App Preferences: Analysing which apps are most frequently used and exploring the psychological motivations behind those choices. App preferences are a pivotal facet of mobile phone usage analysis, offering a profound understanding of users' digital behaviour by examining which applications are most frequently used and the underlying psychological motivations that drive these choices.

Frequent App Usage: This aspect of analysis focuses on identifying the specific applications that users interact with most frequently. By

159

quantifying the time spent on each app and the frequency of launches, analysts can pinpoint the user's favourite and most valuable apps. Frequent app usage can encompass a wide range of categories, from communication and social media to productivity and entertainment apps. Beyond usage statistics, delving into the psychological motivations behind app choices provides deeper insights. It involves exploring why individuals gravitate toward particular apps. These motivations can be multifaceted:

- Functional Utility: Users may select apps that serve essential functions in their daily lives, such as messaging, email, or navigation. These choices are often driven by practicality and efficiency. Look at the way apps are arranged on the home screen, if indeed they are arranged at all. Anything from grouped categories to certain apps on certain pages is telling of practicality and efficiency in the phone's use.

- Emotional Gratification: Some apps offer emotional satisfaction and gratification. Social media platforms, for example, provide avenues for social connection, validation, and entertainment. Users turn to these apps to fulfil emotional needs. However it is important to note that now, there are certain social media apps that come with a degree of stigma given the type of client that populates their servers. 4Chan is a popular one for the darker and angrier sides of everything from fandom to current affairs. In the same way that someone who tells you they eat a lot of McDonalds vs someone who tells you they eat a lot from Waitrose will present very different social identities, so too will the frequent

160

users of Discord and Tumblr when compared to Instagram. So from our side it can be worth investigating this information beforehand to add to the palace and better equip you for your reads of someone's apps.

- Productivity and Self-Improvement: Productivity apps, educational tools, and self-improvement platforms cater to users' aspirations for personal growth and achievement. Motivations here stem from a desire for progress and skill development. Everything from the fitness likes of Centr, Myfitness Pal and Team RH to lumosity and Audible. These insights alone can tell you about how invested in their lives someone is. Of course, too many of them may also suggest a difficulty in sticking to the routines but still possessing a desire, however that is something else entirely.

- Entertainment and Escape: Gaming, streaming, and content consumption apps offer an escape from the demands of daily life. Users turn to these apps for relaxation, entertainment, and stress relief. We are really looking at the volume of apps when compared to others. YouTube and Netflix amongst an array of others from different backgrounds is something I would consider 'normal'. Though when someone has around 30 apps in total and 10 of them are for entertainment then we have cause to gather inferences about their capacity to take part in their own lives. Especially when they are extensions of home gaming systems.

User Behaviour Analysis: Analysing app preferences enables the creation of user profiles based on their digital habits. These profiles

161

can reveal unique characteristics, interests, and lifestyle choices. For instance, a user who frequently engages with fitness and nutrition apps may be health-conscious, while someone who spends considerable time on news and finance apps may have a strong interest in current affairs and financial markets.

What do you see when the home screen is open? This would apply to tablets as well, just as much as it would apply to phones. Pretty much anything that allows the downloads of Apps really. You would be best served in this area if your basic knowledge of apps went a little beyond social media, YouTube, Netflix and whatever email service is in use. We can't always account for the person in question to have categorised their apps in terms of purpose and use. Not everyone will be that degree of obsessive.....nope.......nobody is like that.....I couldn't think of anyone.....

There is little that I can offer in the way of wisdom in this area, suffice to say that when you come across something that you don't recognise or have not used before, you would be wise to engage your curiosity to make sure that the details of it are something that you can take with you moving forward. Given that we live in the age of the need for a Digital Detox and addiction of sorts to the devices we carry with us, exploring the effects of excessive mobile phone use, as well as strategies for reducing screen time and potential addiction would make sense for the deductionist to pay close attention to. As Johann Hari explains in his book Stolen Focus, it is more than simply removing our devices from the immediacy of our location. We need to prevent ourselves from being able to scratch the itch of connection to internet based activity. App preference analysis also plays a role in evaluating the impact of mobile phone usage on users' well-being. It helps identify potential issues, such as excessive social media consumption or smartphone addiction, and provides insights for promoting healthier digital behaviours.

Here are a few apps that would provide some insight into the requirement for digital detox, or at the very least an assistance with curbing access to other areas of the online world as a way to maintain focus on whatever tasks are being worked on by the individual in question:

Freedom - Allows you to block distracting websites and apps for set periods of time. You can schedule recurring 'Freedom Sessions' for when you need to focus.

Forest - Grow virtual trees while you stay off your phone. If you leave the app, the tree dies, providing motivation to stay focused.

Space - Blocks distracting apps and websites of your choosing for pre-set blocks of time.

Offtime - Tracks and limits your device usage with detailed analytics. Can schedule 'Offtime Hours' to restrict apps.

Flipd - Completely locks your phone for a set duration when you need no distractions. No take-backs until the timer runs out.

AppDetox - Blocks your usage of selected apps after you exceed your self-set daily limits.

Freedom Phone - A minimalist 'dumb phone' designed specifically for digital detoxes with no apps or internet.

Screen Time (iOS) - Apple's built-in tool for limiting app usage. Can schedule downtime when apps are blocked.

Digital Wellbeing (Android) - Google's native app for monitoring and restricting phone usage and apps.

It's worth noting that the study of mobile phone psychology is a relatively new and evolving field, and its findings contribute to a deeper understanding of how technology influences human behaviour and psychological well-being. We are really looking at consumer patterns and their implementation within the life of whatever culture you find yourself working within.

Romanticising Wear and Tear

The dangerous tightrope that we walk with using information of this kind, in any situation, is the want to 'feel' like the detective in the funny hat. The same can be said of anything in this arena really that is very niche or not an obvious observation to make. If you feel yourself stepping into something that even closely resembles that, then give yourself a break right away. That is the presentation of ego and however small the showing of this might be, it is kryptonite to your future development with material of this nature.

The reason I mention this in the phone chapter is due to the pastiche of the original pocket watch deduction that was seen in the BBC version with mobile phones. So will you always see a drunk's phone that has scratches on and around the charging cable? No. You may rarely even see an alcoholic with a phone at all, by virtue of the nature of the addiction itself.

Broken or cracked screen protectors are a sign of a clumsy person. Broken or cracked screens can just be a sign of a single event having occurred and not a continued exposure. The screen protector being someone recognising the need for such an add on. The size of the cracks and/or the origin point of the initial impact saying something about the amount of times the screen had been hit can give you an idea as to the frequency of this. However with multiple cracks it can become a challenge to examine a singular origin of impact on a cursory glance. It is better for the speed of your assessments to simply say that the phone is not very well taken care of. If you know the model and can make a fair inductively reasoned assessment as to its expense then this would tell you a little more about the relevance of this within the subject's life.

The point is to not obsess within the small confines of these observations because you are simply trying to look smarter than someone else. If you have the time to make this assessment by virtue of whatever circumstance you are in then by all means do so but these opportunities are few and far between.

The Adventure of Needles and Pictures

"It's not a thing to have a tattoo in, unless you wish to acknowledge that your life is at an end." - The Adventure of the Engineer's Thumb

If you have ever seen any recent image of me, it should be no secret that I love tattoos. I have loads! My arms, my back, my chest and my calves are all very much on their way to being covered. I still find it funny how tattoos are perceived in general. My wife once referred to my Hand tattoo as the international job stopper after getting rejected from a police force position on the back of it. Even though, not 2 weeks later I was hired to run a series of trainings and seminars for them. We have all seen tattoos on people, whether they be plentiful or diminutive, hidden or in plain sight so it would only make sense for us to cover this chapter again and in a little more detail than before. Though even with the first iteration, there was a lot of detail to ingest there too so I hope you have done your homework as they say.

Brief focus on why I have found them to be a gift!

If someone were to ask you 'What is a tattoo?' What would you say? If I might restrict your answer further, it is not to connect to some personal opinion of what they are. A tattoo is a permanent mark or design made on the skin using ink or pigments. Tattoos are created by injecting the ink or pigments into the dermis layer of the skin, which is located just below the outer layer (epidermis). This process is typically performed by a professional tattoo artist using a needle or a tattoo machine. Even with that, just stop for a second and think about what getting one actually means. Permanence, pain (relatively speaking) and expense. Realistically speaking, that is not something that someone enters into flippantly and also means that the artists themselves would have measures in place to review these concerns. Connecting this idea, means that whatever the tattoo is, the strength of meaning must correlate. Even if it is a joke tattoo.

Tattoos can take a multitude of forms, including symbols, images, words, or abstract designs, and they are often chosen by individuals for personal, cultural, artistic, or symbolic reasons. Tattoos have been a part of human culture and history for thousands of years, with different societies and cultures having their own unique traditions and meanings associated with tattooing. So we could take an easy way of developing our understanding here (easy from a relative position) by learning about these cultures and the various social intonations that change around the world. Time consuming but easy enough and if you have a sufficient enough memory palace then you will be able to use this information at a moment's notice. Now in me phrasing it this way, I am not, by any stretch of the imagination, diminishing this level of research at all. This should form part of your everyday practices and the moments wherever you have time. Just because it is something that is already out there and available to you at a moment's notice, I am encouraging you to favour the processes as laid out here for you.

Tattoos can serve a wide range of purposes, from self-expression and body art to commemorating important life events, honouring loved ones, or conveying personal beliefs and values. Due to their permanence, getting a tattoo is a significant decision, and individuals often carefully consider the design and placement of their tattoo before undergoing the procedure. Additionally, advances in tattoo technology have made it possible to remove tattoos through laser tattoo removal, although this process can be costly and may not completely erase the tattoo. It has become something that has drastically addressed the 'risk' involved with the changing of one's mind in relation to the tattoo's that someone has.

Given the wide range of areas that we can consider in the reading of this particular topic, how best then to proceed? How am I best to serve you guys and make sure that there is a system in place that you can use so that no matter the level of background information you are bringing to someone's tattoo's, you will always be able to observe and learn. It is to have a governing set of heuristics that you will be able to utilise at a moment's notice. Something that regardless of that tattoo you see, it will still yield the most information possible. There are only 5 to consider and these are broad enough that you will be able to infer pretty much everything from what it is that you see. We won't go into specifically what the tattoos are, more give you a framework to allow you to discern what it is that you need from the situation.

Where is it?

In these initial stages simply identifying where it is on the body and whether or not it can be covered up is huge. Whether it should be covered up is a different question altogether but given the modern working world and its rather archaic views on this, it is a particularly pertinent question to consider. Some can be covered naturally by virtue of most clothes, some covered by the use of uniform and the rest, no matter what you do, will be on display for all to see. I'm looking at you Post Malone.

Where is it as an initial observation is something to give us insight into the significance of the meaning behind it. This becomes less of a challenge for the smaller tattoo's but before we step into the realms of a Martial Arts class with the '*What if this…*' or '*What if that…*' which could go on for a while.

Take the prime example of an upper arm tattoo of any sort in the bicep, tricep area. Pretty much most uniforms and clothing in general can and do cover this up, and the jobs where the uniform's don't cover this would ultimately mean that, so long as the tattoo is not offensive it would be welcomed anyway. By simple knowledge of this alone we would know that whatever the tattoo is of, it does not affect the subject's life or hinder it in any way for where they are when you observe them. This would ultimately mean that in terms of inferences and further access points of information that we can concentrate entirely on the tattoo and not have to consider any kind of social implication.

In terms of stats and data on this, the representative 'figures' I present here are things I have collected from my years of reading people, case work, getting tattoos and talking to and recording my sessions with tattoo artists. When I met my wife, she managed a Tattoo shop so I had access to many of them. Bicep and upper arm locations are very popular for both men and women. Common bicep/upper arm tattoos for men include tribal designs, biomechanical, Polynesian tribal styles, and anything representing strength, masculinity or power. For women, floral designs, quotes, scripts, butterfly motifs, zodiac symbols, and delicate scrollwork are frequently seen on the upper arm or bicep. Is that meant to draw any kind of gender based insight for you to use? God no! Just common occurrences is all. Even with things like scrollwork and quotes the corollary is still strength but it is less strength in the masculine and more strength in the feminine. Both men and women commonly get tattoo sleeves (covering the entire arm) made up of multiple thematic tattoos. However then we get to question coverage. For example full sleeves in the medical profession are uncommon in general but more common in the porters that work within the hospitals but not doing any medical practice per se.

The tricep area specifically is less common as a primary tattoo location compared to bicep or upper arm. When present, tricep tattoos often continue a sleeve design rather than standing alone. Smaller simple designs like symbols, dates, geometric shapes or words are most prevalent for isolated tricep tattoos. So let us paint a hypothetical example of something that you might see. Let us say that you catch a glimpse of a tattoo on the inner bicep of a woman.

170

It's almost in the shape of a Tarot card and you see it says SELKIE at the bottom of the rectangular shape. If you know what that is already, great but if you don't, here is what you would get from a brief google search.

' Selkies are mythological creatures that can shapeshift between seal and human forms by removing or putting on their seal skin. They feature prominently in the oral traditions and mythology of various cultures, especially those of Celtic and Norse origin. '

Inner biceps would mean that it would be covered by most uniforms and clothes and even more importantly that naturally as the arms hang, it wouldn't be easily seen from that area anyway. You can see from the rest of the arm that the tattoo is not there because of dwindling space from a growing sleeve, it was chosen to go there. We can infer an additional node of a deep, personal tie in here but nothing more at this stage. We can apply our 3 steps here. What stands out from this knowledge alone?

- Shapeshifting between Seal and Human. In other words between the land and the sea.
- Mythology
- Celtic / Norse
- Personal tie ins

Now it should be no secret at this stage, that I am describing someone I know to you. Only so that you will be able to understand how this practice can be used to glean information on a broader scale. The job doesn't have any inferences here but what about if I said to you, if this person had a choice of hobbies that he/she would enjoy pursuing then what would you say those would likely be? There will be a few that fit the criteria. Genuinely do this. From that which stands out above, give any questions you have, life by going through this process now and exploring the information you can use to be able to answer the question I have asked. Are there any thematic concepts coming out from the questions you asked of those 4 points? Even if it is just a preference to doing something inside vs outside or vice versa.

What did you get?......

Don't cheat, as I will tell you in a moment.....
Pretty much anything that involves being outside in nature. Camping, walking, swimming are the main 3 but she will happily settle for anything involving nature. Add this into the fact that due to easy coverage from work uniform there is no additional turmoil for some overly hidden part of who or what she believes herself to be. So if you could ask her one and only one question to be able to have insight into all of this information at once, what would you ask? Read no further and treat this as a light critical thinking exercise and see if you can find something that encapsulates a connection to all of this.

For your approval, may I suggest 'Do you enjoy your job?' or however you would word that question yourself. We are going to cover all areas with a question such as this. Now if you are more focused on the direct assessment of the tattoo itself, you could comment on it

172

and then watch the subject to review how they present it to you. What are their thermo's like? Does this communicate high levels of pride and insight from you noticing something about them which means they get to accent it or is this something else altogether? In terms of where it is, you are looking at the connected topics to tattoo's in terms of their visibility or lack thereof. Any tattoo of the face or head would mean that realistically the job role that they have would come under anything you could label as conventional unless you assign the inductively reasoned observation of a business owner. The only way a head tattoo is getting covered is with a hat and a face tattoo is not getting covered by pretty much anything other than some kind of religious dress or a face mask. Again, I feel the need to reiterate that this isn't a discussion on anything resembling the biases of a workforce. This is more the likelihood of where the personality, that would be motivated to get a tattoo of this kind, would likely gravitate towards.

How Big Is It?

It should be easy to note that if a tattoo is of a particular size and shape then it is more of a challenge to cover. With this I am specifically referencing anything that starts as a half sleeve and gets bigger. The initial conclusion that you might draw is 'Well the bigger the tattoo, the more it means to the person' you would be wrong in this case. In language learning terms this would be a false friend. We can however say that the bigger the tattoo, the more the wearer would be comfortable with talking about its meaning and connections

173

to themselves. Think of me in this instance. You should all be aware of my affinity for Holmes and the connected stories and life. I have a full sleeve that connects all of these together and various other elements like my Deadpool/Sherlock on my leg too. Now, would you say that my fondness for this life would be diminished at all if I just had one small pipe tattooed behind my ear? The answer would be no.

When you think about it, the tattoo size is more of a fondness for the tattoo/art and financial capability than it is a direct connection to the source
material it is based on. The decision to get a tattoo in honour of or connection to something is the real sign of the strength of interest in something. The size of it is more reflective of their life at that time than anything else. It is in this way akin to seeing someone with a regular gym routine. We could make the observation that health and fitness is very important to them and yet it could be equally important to them to work out so they can eat whatever they want when they get home. The gym is a gateway to allow them to get out of food jail, so to speak. I refer you to anything Ricky Gervais has said of his fondness for wine and the reasons as to why he goes running.

Let's take a moment to look at Dave Bautista. The code over there will take you to a video of him talking about his tattoos but just stay here with me for a moment or 2. If you don't know who he is, take a moment to google a picture by all means but don't follow through to the video just yet. All of his tattoos are of a considerable size or they are connected in order to form a tattoo that is of a big size. We can reverse engineer the chain of reasoning as he is a famous man as we know he does not have a conventional job. Nor is he a conventional man. At this stage, with as much or as little as you know, would you deduce him to be a man who is proud of his heritage? Whether you figure him to be simply an American or anything else. Now whatever your answer is, here is a bit of knowledge for you. He has a tattoo that directly connects to his heritage. For however proud or not proud you figured him out to be, how big would you say the tattoo is of this? Not necessarily where it is just the size. Once you have a response to this, then go and watch the video and see if you were right.

In terms of a correlation the tattoo itself is not really as big as how much he feels in his heart for 'where he comes from'. Hopefully this little exercise will go some way to helping you understand this point. To paraphrase the modern phallic remark 'Size isn't everything'. To sum this point up, the size will tell you about the cost and artistic freedom that the person who has the tattoo is in possession of. The bigger the tattoo, the more someone has the financial freedom to be able to push it towards their artistic connections of something they are passionate about without it causing too much concern in other areas of their life. You think of any role or position in life where people have big tattoos and this will be the heuristic and rational process that governs it.

175

Can it be covered?

With this we are looking solely at the placement of the tattoo itself. Tattoos have become increasingly popular and mainstream in Western societies over the past few decades. With this growing acceptance, there has been a shift in the symbolic meaning and placement of tattoos. In the past, tattoos were often associated with subcultures like bikers, sailors, or prisoners. Tattoos would be prominently displayed on areas like the forearms, hands, or neck as a sign of commitment to a group or lifestyle. Nowadays, tattoos are sported by people from all walks of life. Discrete tattoos in areas that can be covered up, like the back, chest, or upper arms have become more common.

The location and visibility of a tattoo today is often a personal choice, not necessarily tied to the meaning behind the artwork. Some professional settings still frown upon visible tattoos, so ink in coverable spots allows people to conceal them when needed. Other people may get meaningful tattoos in openly visible areas as a form of self-expression. For example, tattoos supporting social or political causes placed on the forearm make a bold statement. Meanwhile, matching tattoos for couples or families are often inked over the heart or on the wrist. Take for example the story of my hand tattoo. Though the meaning is nothing even closely resembling anything offensive, it was still not allowed as part of the work culture I desired to be a part of. Though in terms of the work force, I am accepted as a singular entity because it is not anything directly connected to the force in question.

Tattoos today are more about personal meaning and style than about outward projection of a subculture identity. Both concealed and conspicuous placements have become widely accepted in mainstream Western society. The location of a tattoo is now an individual decision, weighed by the symbolism of the artwork and the level of discretion desired in professional or social settings. Whether displayed openly or not, tattoos allow people to assert their beliefs, commemorate loved ones, or decorate their skin however they choose. For our work here we would be wise to consider coverage in direct connection to the context we are seeing someone in. If you think of a teacher, of any age group, with a visible tattoo that you can see when observing them in a school, it is entirely different to seeing them in a coffee shop. Even if they are wearing the same clothes. The context surrounding the visibility is going to give you different information to work with. One may tell you more about the location than the person and vice versa.

Visibility through clothing should also be considered. Some tattoos can be seen through most light coloured clothing, depending on the thickness of the material. What is that to say of the information that the visibility of the tattoo communicates? It would be the same as our original deductions, just a more watered down version. For example, let's take a moment to look at David Beckham. For those that don't know who he is, you are welcome to google him. Suffice to say, he is a heavily tattooed person. A man known for his fondness of the world of fashion. Maybe through his wife, but that is an argument for another day. White is something that he would frequently have to wear with his suits of choice and also with the majority of kits and sporting attire that he had to work in. I am picking on white coloured clothes as they are the easiest to turn transparent under heat and moisture as well as the projections of colour from the tattoos underneath if the shirt is of a thin material. Exploring coverage with this, anything created by virtue of the sports kit by itself, is not something he would decide and so anything that would be visible through the clothing during games and training would indicate the priority of the matters at hand and that the adding of tattoo's to the body of footballers does not really mean anything within the grand scheme of things and is not viewed the same as say, an insurance company.

The same can be said of the tattoos connected to these fashion events so we can abduce a corollary of information here. Just a small qualifier, the abductive observation is about to be stated in the context of someone that doesn't know who David Beckham is. Coverage would give us a job area that is accepting of large scale tattoos and therefore they all must be of a non-controversial nature. So can it be covered would be yes and no. This would depend on whether you would view him as having one very large tattoo or a series of tattoos that cover a large area. How big it is gives us the notion of how much it would cost and therefore an idea as to how much he has in the way of disposable income that he can put towards tattoos. Even more of an idea if you are capable of recognizing specific artists and their work. Much in the same way that you can discern visual differences between Picasso and Manet. Where it is would cover all manner of emblems from the information that he wants to be able to show the world. Don't worry so much about piecing all this together now as we will tackle a case study on all of this in the next few pages. Let's not forget that these are based on the assessments of simply that there are tattoos. It doesn't account for exactly what they are at this stage. So when you notice this too it will bolster your observations further.

How much would it hurt?

An arguably crucial decision in the commitment to any tattoo. There is a general rule of thumb in that all humans like to live in relativistic comfort. Conversely, this is the avoidance of pain. Now it goes without saying that all tattoos hurt. This, as I say though, is a relative term. Relative to the person and the reason for the tattoo itself. Given the natural structure of the body, there will be some areas that hurt more than others. The dorsum of the foot, cubital fossa or the neck being the most common but when you step into the areas of eyes, eyelids and soles of the feet, this becomes less common but more obvious.

Psychoanalytic theory offers some insights into why people may enjoy or feel comfortable getting tattoos. The experience of getting a tattoo involves enduring pain and discomfort. According to psychologists as far back as Freud or currently this would be people like David J. Linden - Neuroscientist at Johns Hopkins University. His research examines the neurobiology of pleasure, focusing on the role of the nucleus accumbens and neurotransmitters like dopamine. He is the author of the book The Compass of Pleasure. The human psyche has innate drives toward both pleasure and aggression. Getting a tattoo allows an individual to express unconscious aggressive or masochistic impulses in a socially acceptable way. The pain involved also releases endorphins that can produce a pleasurable high. As such, the pain of getting a tattoo may provide both gratification and catharsis. This would be lessened in terms of the 'meatier' areas of the body and become more solely about the art itself.

The interaction between tattoo artist and client involves a significant degree of intimacy and trust. The tattoo recipient projects feelings and motivations onto the tattoo artist, while the artist expresses care through the delicate tattooing process. This bonding experience provides comfort through transference. The tattoo artist symbolically takes on roles like a caring parent or friend. A modern day bartender, who instead of wiping the inside of a glass with a pristine white cloth, would colour you in with needles and listen to your problems, thoughts and insights into the world. A tattoo permanently transforms the body in a controlled way chosen by the recipient. This can allow people to reassert feelings of control and mastery over their bodies. The permanence also provides ongoing comfort as a symbolic act of commitment to one's self-identity or values. Tattoos can represent a defining moment or ideal that the bearer wants to hold onto. This is especially highlighted in areas that would actively cause more unquestionable pain.

Psychoanalysts see tattoos as fulfilling fundamental human drives. They offer a mix of pain and pleasure, a bonding interaction, and a chance to control one's self-narrative. For willing recipients, these factors provide comfort and enjoyment throughout the tattoo process. Neuroscience also offers some explanations for why people may enjoy or feel comfortable getting tattoos. The experience of getting a tattoo activates the body's pain pathways, releasing endorphins that act as natural painkillers and induce feelings of pleasure. The rush of endorphins can lead to a high or rush, which some find enjoyable.

The brain's reward system is also activated by tattooing. Areas like the nucleus accumbens and amygdala process the experience as rewarding, reinforcing continued engagement in the activity. The anticipation before the tattoo session also engages reward circuits. Social bonding with the tattoo artist activates dopamine receptors, as human connection is intrinsically tied to the brain's reward system. The shared experience may also reinforce bonds with fellow group members in the case of matching tattoos. For those inclined toward sensation-seeking and novelty, the process of getting a tattoo and permanently modifying one's appearance generates excitement and interest. The brain's drive for novelty and new experiences is engaged. The process of getting a tattoo forces focus on the present moment. This acts as a form of mindfulness meditation, with reduced worrying about the past or future. Lowering stress can provide comfort and mood enhancement.

We can look at the area in context with whether or not someone has any 'available space' i.e. any other tattoos in and around that area. With this, we are really looking at the choice to move towards a painful area for a tattoo or not. Take my most recent tattoo for example, in my elbow crease. I wanted something there to finish off the sleeve on my left arm. I will try and communicate this to you as bluntly as this current stream will allow....

I F****** HATED EVERY SECOND OF IT

To be clear, I love my tattoo. I believe it to be gorgeous and works really well with the rest of the images but had I not gotten anything here then there would be this big obvious gap in the images on my arm. Other people may not have noticed it but I did. I went into that sitting knowing full well that I would be in pain for the 4 hours I was there. The remaining space dictated my choice to get the tattoo there. As such, the meaning is not in relation to any psychoanalytical suggestion and was only communicated by the overall piece itself.

Whereas if you look at British Rapper Professor Green and his neck tattoo. This actually relates to being stabbed in the neck during a mugging incident in 2009. The attack left him hospitalised with serious injuries. After recovering, he got the word "Lucky" tattooed on his neck at the location of the stabbing. This signified feeling fortunate to have survived such a life-threatening assault. This is quite big for a neck tattoo and would be in a painful place that is not as a result of continued work in other areas. Therefore the meaning will have an added connection to the placement in a lot of cases.

What is it of?

The most obvious of all the heuristics to consider when looking at tattooing and is the reason I left it to the end. What is it of, seems to fall into a category of potential invisibility. So we look at it here as a way of keeping everyone accountable. This is one of those areas of research that could be explained very easily, broaden your symbology and imagery knowledge as a matter of continued building within your memory palace. Simply noticing the other elements that exist within the bigger picture as well will help the details to grow within the development of the overall deduction breakdown you make.

Now most of these elements were covered in the first iteration of this series but so that we can build on this breakdown, there are a number of easily researchable areas to go through when it is in reference to the cultural variations of the same themes. Looking at numbers that will be featured on people. This could be dates, times or both. You could look at how different cultures around the world would show a date. The easy difference is between the USA and the UK. So if you were to see a date breakdown in this way:

05.21.11

What would that indicate? Something happening on May 21st right? But also a connection to America. You can build these extra steps into your breakdown to give you more information than at the surface of the observations you make. Clocks are a prevalent feature of

183

memorial tattoos around the world. Not anything digital but clocks with an actual face. Let us imagine that you see a time that you could read as 10:14. How many different ways could that be reinvented?

- 10:14 am
- October 14th

Looking at a rational breakdown of information, how many different big moments that exist in someone's life are represented by a time? Looking right across the board it is normally a birth or a death. Looking at the clock in context with whatever else is there would give some insight as to which way that is leaning. The date gives you a much broader net to cast and would need to direct your information in the context of other pieces of information.

Let's put all of these together in context with a picture of someone's

tattoo. I will prompt you with certain questions you might ask, or even certain observations you might make. Please bear in mind though that anything else you come up with should always be taken into account as well.

This is someone's right leg. This is the front part of their shin. They had to roll their trouser leg up in order to take the picture for me to use here but this should also be more than enough in order to contextualise this completely for you.

- **Where is it?** The details of which have been covered in the context of the photo from the last paragraph. However, the right leg within this photo also contains a glimpse as to the other leg as well. Are these going to be something that would be viewed in the job /he/she has? Is it covered all the time or just for work? Does this spill over to any time that this person would consider to be play?

- **How big is it?** Each individual tattoo is not that big but can you see any theme that would join them or are they a series of separate images? In addition to that, are there a series of themes each with their own individual elements within them? The themes may give you an idea as to the separate collective sizes, if indeed you see that there are any at all.

- **Can it be covered?** Well, can it? If the legs are something that can be covered, have they been chosen over the arms or anywhere else? If so, why? If not, why not?

- **How much would it hurt?** Depending on the knowledge that you are bringing to the table when reading this, you may need some additional research to be able to answer that at this stage, or even to have had some tattoo's yourself. You may get by with a well-reasoned inductively determined answer following feeling your own legs. Once you have answered that question you can look into the possible motivations for why this person has chosen the legs for these images over anywhere else.

- **What is it of?** First off, you may not recognise any of it. In which case, you may need to go through some additional steps of research. If you do then this will raise additional questions. For example if you were to see a pipe and/or a sherlock Holmes quote on someone's leg, are they fans of Holmes, the connected symbolic information or both?

After having gone through all of these steps you would now have a multitude of statements, answers and inquiries to make if were you able to meet this person in real life. Now, once you have gone through all of the information from the first edition and then from this one as well you will have an unstoppable amount of information to use whenever it is that you notice someone's tattoo.

Art in the blood is liable to take the strangest forms after all so now that we have a road map with which to navigate this journey we have to ask ourselves, is it really going to be as strange anymore? Now that you know what to look for and how to break this down into its finite parts it will no longer read as something curious, more along the lines of a series of steps to take in order to get you to where you need to go.

More Than Mr. Turner's Thumb

"I had come to an entirely erroneous conclusion which shows, my dear Watson, how dangerous it always is to reason from insufficient data." The Boscombe Valley Mystery

Something to concern ourselves with first is the process of critical and deductive thinking in general. Whether this be syllogistic, propositional, modus tollens or anything else in between. If you are bringing unsound information and details to the table then the outcome you can bring will be challenged by default. Now there are many different ways to compute the journey of a successful outcome from the basis of a strong premise and what sound or unsound reasoning can do along the way. What we can, nay, should be concerning ourselves with in the earlier stages of our information harvesting is the strength, significance and accuracy of the data we have been able to obtain.

The next few points are not to try and insight any tin foil hat wearing madness. Just merely a few thoughts on the way many people seem to operate when it comes to thinking a little more critically about the information they have at their disposal. For those that aren't familiar with Jonathan Pie, this is a comedian from the UK whose rants started off being a mixture of rather clever and verbose insults mixed with a politically satirical twist. It was initially about highlighting the growing ridiculousness of matters in the UK. The design being that it was supposed to be funny at its core. With each new video that he releases, it has stopped being funny, or rather stopped being as funny and started being concerning and at times even a little depressing.

Why would we critically reason that to be?

In simple terms it is when people stop accepting the comedic nature of what is being spoken about and actually look into what the comedian is saying if it isn't popular to already be common knowledge and even then, how are we as the ignorant public looking to verify that? Are we reading an article that says there have been studies, or are we going to the studies themselves for the data? Even when we get to the studies, how are we evaluating the information being put forth? I would refer to the work of Vincent Denault within the realms of the plight of pseudoscience on YouTube. I always try to be as clear as I can about the information I am talking about and do my best to make sure that the connections are readily available to all who wish to make them. There is an almost relaxed empiricism that exist within the realms of knowledge sharing if I may borrow the analogy from British comedian Bill Bailey, who when talking of the work of Stephen Hawking jokingly made the point that he was prepared to accept what Dr. Hawking said of the world based on knowing the kind of work he did and how far beyond Bill's capacity it was. With all information, including the details in this book, I actively encourage people to test it out and worry less about the 'if it's on the internet then it must be true' kind of approach. Test it all and explore the veracity of all connected details from everywhere and above all else when it comes to comedy, let's appreciate a joke for what it is and the use of satire in an attempt to try and prove, or at the very least, make a point.

188

With that in mind, let's get on to the hands!....

Exchange and beyond

Hands. We all have them and we shouldn't be ashamed of them. They are more often than not the vehicles that are used to exchange all manner of data with another. Whether this be in the giving of items, the shaking of hands or the communication of some kind of personal care routine. These are the implements that whether we like it or not, are a function of a majority of our communication and as human beings we can't not communicate. So if we think of these in terms of our Therapists theory. What can we view the closer we get to someone's hands and how does this change the observable information that we can glean as a result.

Take something like idle or restless hands. There are a number of common medical/psychological causes for this:

- Restless legs syndrome (RLS): RLS is a neurological disorder that causes an uncontrollable urge to move the legs, often accompanied by uncomfortable sensations. It is the most common cause of restless hands.
- Attention deficit hyperactivity disorder (ADHD): ADHD is a neurodevelopmental disorder characterised by inattention, hyperactivity, and impulsivity. People with ADHD often have restless hands and fidget.
- Parkinson's disease: Parkinson's disease is a neurodegenerative disorder that affects movement. People

with Parkinson's disease may experience restless hands, tremors, and stiffness.

- Essential tremor: Essential tremor is a neurological disorder that causes involuntary shaking of the hands, head, or voice. People with essential tremor may experience restless hands especially when they are trying to perform tasks that require fine motor skills.
- Anxiety disorders: Anxiety disorders, such as generalised anxiety disorder and social anxiety disorder, can cause a variety of physical symptoms, including restless hands.
- Depression: Depression can also cause a variety of physical symptoms, including restless hands.
- Stress: Stress can trigger the release of hormones that can cause restless hands.
- Boredom: Boredom can also lead to restless hands, as people may fidget or tap their fingers to keep themselves occupied.
- Stimulant use: Caffeine and other stimulant drugs can cause restless hands.
- Lack of sleep: Sleep deprivation can also lead to restless hands.

Restless hands is a common condition that can affect people of all ages. It is estimated that up to 15% of the population experiences restless hands at some point in their lives. Restless hands can be a nuisance, but it is usually not a serious medical condition. I for one have a shaking nature to my left hand. This has been a part of who I am since I was very young. I have had it checked out many times with no definitive diagnosis on the reasons behind why it is there. However when you look at the available causes, of which I am sure there are many more. The ones I have collected here for you appear to be the most common. There are a few that could match my lifestyle and give you information to explore further with someone like me. I have been assessed for ADHD, I have had depression before, I do get bored very easily with a number of things, I do drink coffee and I am an insomniac. All you have done so far is noticed that there is a restlessness to one of my hands and now you have a number of inferences with which to explore. Hence my reasoning for a brief discussion surrounding critical thought at the beginning of this chapter.

However, if you have restless hands that are severe or interfere with your daily activities, you should see a doctor to rule out any underlying medical conditions. Treatment for restless hands will depend on the underlying cause. For example, if restless hands are caused by RLS, medication may be prescribed. If restless hands are caused by stress, relaxation techniques may be helpful. For you as the deducer of information in these scenarios it will be up to you to become as familiar with the base knowledge in each of these areas as possible. For example, the shakes from withdrawals of sorts are very different to stimulant use, as they are to sleep deprivation. There are behavioural reflections that one could use to make further inferences in these areas when you start to assess what each of these could possibly connect to. When you think of something as workaday as lack of sleep, how might one modify their behaviour over the next day in order to cope with this? You can explore the connections to this and then expand them out further. Like ripples in a pond.

Nailed it

A much maligned social observation in seeing someone that bites their nails. What are we truly seeing when someone does that though? Can you describe it in full? Or is your answer that it's dirty and your reasoning behind it, words to the effect of 'well it just is'. There are a number of psychological reasons why someone might bite their nails. Some of the most common reasons include:

- Anxiety: Nail biting can be a way of coping with stress and anxiety. The repetitive behaviour can be calming and can help to take the mind off of worries.
- Boredom: Nail biting can also be a way to relieve boredom or to keep the hands occupied.
- Perfectionism: People with perfectionist tendencies may bite their nails as a way to express their frustration or disappointment with themselves.
- Habit: Nail biting can also be a simple habit that people learn from a young age and that is difficult to break.

A number of studies have investigated the psychological reasons for nail biting. One study, published in the journal of Anxiety Disorders, found that people who bite their nails are more likely to experience anxiety and stress than people who do not bite their nails. Another study, published in the Clinical Psychology Review, found that nail biting is associated with a number of other psychological disorders, including obsessive-compulsive disorder (OCD), attention deficit hyperactivity disorder (ADHD), and tic disorder. So in this hypothetical, you notice someone that bites their nails and you have, thanks to your memory palace, a list of available and verifiable pieces of information with which to explore their effects in the world that you are observing. Now you are in a better position with which to analyse the data in front of you and its connections towards other observable traits that you can see. A hangnail is also connected to the inferences that can be made here. This is a small piece of skin that tears away from the corner of the nail. It is often caused by dry skin or by picking at the cuticle. Hangnails can be painful and can lead to infection if they are not properly cared for.

Here are some of the most common defects in the human fingernails, in addition to hangnails and nail biting that you can add to your data banks as you grow:

- Beau's lines: These are horizontal ridges or grooves that run across the nail plate. They can be caused by illness, trauma, or malnutrition.
- Clubbing: This is a condition in which the nails thicken and curve around the fingertips. It can be a sign of lung disease, heart disease, or other serious health conditions. I would opt to look up some images of this online to truly get a sense of what clubbing is and what it looks like.
- Onycholysis: A condition in which the nail separates from the nail bed. It can be caused by trauma, infection, or certain

medications. A common occurrence for teenagers and those that work in construction.

- Pitting: This is a condition in which small pits or dents appear in the nail plate. It can be caused by psoriasis, eczema, or other skin conditions.
- Ridges: These are vertical lines that run down the nail plate. They can be caused by ageing, trauma, or certain medications. I am not looking to provide the list here as it would just be a space filler and something that you can easily review in available texts.
- Terry's nails: This is a condition in which the nails become white and translucent, except for a narrow pink band at the tip. It can be a sign of liver disease, heart disease, or diabetes.
- Yellow nail syndrome: This is a condition in which the nails become yellow and thickened. It can be caused by lung disease, lymphatic disease, or certain medications.
- Brittle nails: These are nails that are thin and easily break or split. They can be caused by ageing, dry weather, or certain medications.
- Ingrown nails: These are nails that curve inwards and grow into the surrounding skin. They can be painful and can lead to infection.
- Leukonychia: This is a condition in which the nails become white or opaque. It can be caused by trauma, infection, or certain medications.

- Mees' lines: These are white horizontal bands that run across the nail plate. They can be caused by trauma, arsenic poisoning, or certain medications.
- Onychomadesis: This is a condition in which the entire nail plate falls off. It can be caused by trauma, infection, or certain medications.
- Paronychia: This is an infection of the skin around the nail. It can be caused by bacteria, yeast, or fungi.

Is this an intellectual flex or subtle encouragement for you to move into some kind of dermatological practice? Neither really. I am looking for it to be demonstrative of the approach to the critical analysis of observable traits in context with the degree of information you can bring to the analysis of what it is that you have seen. If you take something like the observation of brittle nails, you could bring all of the connected information to the fore for your examination and interaction with the person in question. Alternatively you could review the information behind what modern medical practice agrees to be a standard healthy nail. There are traits that bridge gender, ethnicity and culture to get to agreed upon traits. That way if you were to see anything that deviates from these traits you would know them to be deficient in a subset of areas but in a generalised manner. Still good information to work with but should be enough to illustrate the points I am trying to make....hopefully.

With the hands, they are in a unique position to be able to offer insight into the reflections of repetition. Think about something as seemingly innocuous as using a pen. A pen of any sort bear in mind.

Now if you are in a position or job role that requires the use of a pen everyday then there is a very high possibility that your hands, in particular your dominant one will reflect that. Even more so if this is a fountain pen but the frequency with which they are used nowadays has wildly diminished. How about more appropriately, the keyboard? With the number of people working from home and in remote job roles increasing, these are the repetitive conditions that the hands are very often put through. Though keyboards are more reflective in the wrists than in the hands, it is the constant repetitive action that can cause these areas to reflect their use. I presume many of you are familiar with the term 'repetitive strain injury'. The most common office based ailments are as follows:

- Carpal tunnel syndrome (CTS) is a condition that occurs when the median nerve that runs through the carpal tunnel in the wrist is compressed. This can cause pain, numbness, and tingling in the hand and fingers. CTS is the most common RSI, and it is particularly common in office workers who spend a lot of time typing and using a mouse. Also very popular with drummers.
- Tendonitis is inflammation of a tendon, which is a cord that attaches muscle to bone. Tendinitis can affect any tendon in the body, but it is most common in the hands, wrists, elbows, and shoulders. Office workers are at risk of tendonitis from repetitive tasks such as typing, mousing, and lifting objects. Poor manual handling practices too.
- Tennis elbow is a type of tendonitis that affects the tendons on the outside of the elbow. It is caused by overuse of the

196

forearm muscles, which are used to extend the wrist and fingers. Tennis elbow is common in athletes who play tennis, but it can also occur in office workers who perform repetitive tasks such as typing and using a mouse.

- Trigger finger is a condition that causes a finger or thumb to lock in a bent position. It is caused by inflammation of the tendon sheath, which is a tube that surrounds the tendon. Trigger finger is common in office workers who perform repetitive tasks such as typing and using a mouse.

Now as much as this may seem like a list of potential injury woes for the hypochondriacs of the world, there are very few people that consider the implications of a lack of care when working for extended periods of time behind a desk. I would argue that this would very likely be why we saw a rise of standing desks and walking pads during the global effects of lockdowns around the world. People noticed a change in their body that, though minor in size, could have an effect over time and took steps to mitigate this as they had very little else to do.

Given the lack of awareness (a pandemic in and of itself) that people have in the way of personal care to this degree and combine that with the knowledge of the virtual overpopulation of 'desk' jobs, this can give us some insight into other possible causes that would be easy to spot in the individuals that we encounter on a daily basis.

When we start to put all of these ideas together it becomes a very real possibility that we could deduce a trade worker of sorts by a mere handshake or the fingernails of someone that doesn't drink enough water because they smoke too much. Continuing the job role dynamic here and in order to build up our knowledge of the effects that certain roles can have on the hands we can take a look at a glossary of roles that can be found pretty much anywhere online. You could even ask one of the many AI services that exist now to generate you a list of common job roles within a specific area of the world. This in turn would allow you to abductively understand the implications of effects to the hands.

To cite a classic example, take a McDonald's worker of some sort. I am using this as an example as I used to work there years ago and consequently I can spot a fellow kitchen crew member from a mile away. Consider what you know of the role at this stage. It might be as surfaced based as them cooking and serving a specific range of foods. Thinking a little bit more on it, you may get to the idea that there is some sort of cleaning regime that would have to be adhered to, owing to the fact that this is a restaurant business after all and subject to the scrutiny of health and safety practices. How would you go about finding out something more specific? Therefore improving the accuracy of any observations you can make about the hands of a fast food worker because you can bring more knowledge to the table. To paraphrase Holmes. How durable are the bricks you can make from the clay you are using?

Think of the practice of 'flipping a burger'. This is nothing like doing this on a barbeque from home. Imagine a lid of sorts that comes down from the top to cook the meat from the top and the bottom at the same time. Keeping to the fast element of fast food. Now, when I was there, the timer was set to just over 3 minutes for a run of 8 pieces of meat. Now you don't have to be a chef to understand that in order to cook the meat safely, that would mean the metal for the grill has to be hot enough to burn you. A spatula and tongs are used to remove the meat from the grill but there are no gloves used in the removal here. So as the burgers cook there will be an adhesive grease to the top platter of the grill that can drop off onto the backs of the hands of those that frequently work in the kitchen. The grill is scraped and wiped down frequently but dealing with heat and speed, these types of burn patterns are a frequent occurrence. Even down to thin burn lines on the back of the hand near the wrist where the grill has been cleaned under speed. The smells of those that work on the tills, fries, the kitchen or even as the humble janitor are all wildly different based on the fact that it is based in a hot environment and the individuals will have to interact with a specific set of items and cleaning products over time. The sweat acts as a catalyst of sorts for the odours of the environment.

There is a romanticised notion of observation that sits within this category as well. Spotting a pilot by their left thumb being one of the major culprits here thanks to the TV show. Yet there is some truth to the elements of a singular thumb when observing a pilot but in order to get anywhere close to sure of the vocation one would need to acknowledge the requirement for a very specific context. Uniforms, insignia, being in an airport. The thumb alone is far too small of an insight with way too many variables to consider by itself. This presents an interesting angle to our understanding of reflections in the hands over time and that the observations we make are inexorably linked to the knowledge we bring to the table. So as a critical thinking exercise, what could be considered the differences between the hands of a cellist and the hands of someone that plays the bass guitar? We won't consider the upright bass for now.

Some things to consider:

- Are they played in the same way?
- Are the strings the same size between each instrument?
- How do left vs right handed people differ when playing each of the instruments?
- Does it help to be a specific height or build when playing these?
- Are different sized cello's/bass guitars a thing? If so, why?

Whether you know the answers to these questions or whether you don't, in sourcing the information that connects to them you will have a more concrete avenue to explore with the actual person in real life from just looking at their hands. Take the first question at its most fundamental level. One uses a bow and the other does not, one is traditionally played from a seated position with the instrument standing upright and the other is not.

The effects of the bow:

Improved fine motor skills
Fine motor skills are the small, precise movements that we use to manipulate small objects. Playing the cello bow requires a great deal

of fine motor control, as the cellist must be able to move the bow in a controlled and precise manner to produce the desired sound.

A study published in the journal Neuropsychologia found that cellists had better fine motor skills than non-musicians. The study participants were asked to perform a number of tasks, such as threading a needle and pouring water into a narrow cup, and the cellists performed significantly better than the non-musicians.

Increased strength and flexibility

The muscles in the hands and fingers are strengthened and stretched by the act of playing the cello bow. The cellist must use their muscles to hold the bow in position and to move it back and forth across the strings. A study published in the journal Musculoskeletal Science and Practice found that cellists had stronger and more flexible hands than non-musicians. The study participants were asked to perform a number of grip strength and range of motion tests, and the cellists performed significantly better than the non-musicians.

Improved coordination

Playing the cello bow requires a great deal of coordination between the two hands. The cellist must be able to coordinate the movements of their left hand (which is fingering the strings) and their right hand (which is holding the bow) in order to produce a musical sound. A study published in the journal Experimental Brain Research found that cellists had better hand-eye coordination than non-musicians. The study participants were asked to perform a number of tasks, such as catching a ball and threading a needle, and the cellists performed significantly better than the non-musicians.

Reduced pain and stiffness

Playing the cello bow can help to reduce pain and stiffness in the hands. The act of moving the bow back and forth across the strings can help to increase blood flow to the hands and to lubricate the joints. A study published in the journal Arthritis and Rheumatism found that cellists had less pain and stiffness in their hands than non-musicians. The study participants were asked to complete a questionnaire about their hand pain and stiffness, and the cellists reported significantly less pain and stiffness than the non-musicians.

Cello Strings:

Calluses

One of the most obvious effects of cello strings on the hands is the development of calluses. Calluses are thick areas of skin that form in response to repeated friction. When cellists play their instruments, their fingers rub against the strings, which causes calluses to form on the fingertips. Calluses can be painful at first, but they eventually help to protect the skin from further damage. They also help to improve the cellist's grip on the strings, which can lead to improved performance.

Increased blood flow

Playing the cello strings also increases blood flow to the hands. This is because the muscles and tendons in the hands are working hard to press down on the strings. Increased blood flow helps to bring oxygen and nutrients to the hands, which can promote healing and prevent injuries.

Improved dexterity

Playing the cello strings requires a great deal of dexterity. The cellist must be able to move their fingers quickly and accurately in order to produce the desired notes. Cello playing can help to improve dexterity in both the left and right hands. A study published in the journal Neuropsychology found that cellists had better finger dexterity than non-musicians. The study participants were asked to perform a number of tasks, such as picking up small objects and threading a needle, and the cellists performed significantly better than the non-musicians.

Reduced risk of injury

Cello playing can help to reduce the risk of injury to the hands. This is because the muscles and tendons in the hands are strengthened by the act of playing the instrument. Strong muscles and tendons are less likely to be injured. A study published in the journal Musculoskeletal Science and Practice found that cellists had lower rates of hand injuries than non-musicians. The study participants were asked to report any hand injuries that they had sustained in the past year, and the cellists reported significantly fewer injuries than the non-musicians.

Let's compare that to a bass:

Improved fine motor skills

Playing the bass requires a great deal of fine motor control, as the bassist must be able to move their fingers quickly and accurately to pluck the strings. A study published in the journal Neuropsychologia found that bass players had better fine motor skills than non-musicians.

Increased strength and flexibility

The muscles in the hands and fingers are strengthened and stretched by the act of playing the bass. The bassist must use their muscles to pluck the strings and to fret the notes. A study published in the journal Musculoskeletal Science and Practice found that bass players had stronger and more flexible hands than non-musicians.

Improved coordination

Playing the bass requires a great deal of coordination between the two hands. The bassist must be able to coordinate the movements of their left hand (which is fretting the notes) and their right hand (which is plucking the strings) in order to produce a musical sound. A study published in the journal Experimental Brain Research found that bass players had better hand-eye coordination than non-musicians.

Reduced pain and stiffness

Playing the bass can help to reduce pain and stiffness in the hands. The act of plucking the strings and fretting the notes can help to increase blood flow to the hands and to lubricate the joints. A study published in the journal Arthritis and Rheumatism found that bass players had less pain and stiffness in their hands than non-musicians.

There are a few medically proven defects that can occur from playing the bass, but they are relatively rare and can be avoided by taking proper precautions.

- RSI's
- Tendonitis
- Carpal Tunnel Syndrome

To avoid these defects, it is important to take proper precautions when playing the bass. Here are some tips:

- Warm up before playing: Warming up helps to prepare your body for the demands of playing the bass and can help to prevent injuries. A good warm-up should include stretching your hands and fingers, and playing some light exercises.
- Take breaks often: Don't play for more than 30 minutes at a time without taking a break. This will help to prevent your muscles and tendons from becoming fatigued.
- Use proper technique: Make sure you are using proper technique when playing the bass. This will help to avoid putting unnecessary strain on your hands and wrists.
- Adjust your bass: Make sure your bass is properly adjusted to fit your body. This will help to avoid putting unnecessary strain on your hands and wrists.

This is just a generalised approach to separating the information out that exists and comparing the sights that can be seen in the hands of those you are observing, with the degree of information you have stored. In following the reasoning channels of the information

205

connected to these kinds of target areas it will be about understanding what is present when compared with the aspects that are not.

Bass straps set to a lower level will put undue stress on the hands and wrists. If we see a player with a low strap that has no outward signs of stress to that area then we can now ask several questions along the lines of how long have they been playing compared to how long their arms and therefore their reach actually is. Longer than average reach would mean they could comfortably stretch past the point that these stats would suggest without stress and a shorter bass strap may simply be awkward to play, also, stress is felt over time and one inference we could make through this simple observation is that they have not been playing for a long period of time, or long enough to register it as anything other than muscular soreness from inexperience.

You observe someone cooking (odd that you are watching someone cook in this example but just hear me out) and you notice that as they are chopping vegetables, they are looking around the room for their next task and conducting conversations. You know this person to be a musician. We know from the cited information above that there has been research to indicate the dexterity and fine motor control of the hand positions of bassists when compared to non-musical people. Could you confirm a bass player from this? Absolutely not. What you could do is to put it in the remit of instruments that require this type of dextrous control over their small digits. Most stringed instruments and the piano would fit this arena. We are entering into the realms of what my friend and colleague Jim Wenzel would refer to as VDC - Validate, dismiss or clarify. If you think Bass and have information that could connect to this, great. You need to interact with this in order to validate or dismiss your hypothesis. Once completed you will have something that will have been clarified based on the review of the available information in connection to the related data.

Tracing, Tracing, Tracing

"You see, I have a lot of special knowledge which I apply to the problem, and which facilitates matters wonderfully"   A Study in Scarlet

Initially we took a fairly global approach to the tracing of an individual from their looks and their handwriting to knowledge of the local area and any slang that would be used in the regional sense towards specific countries and parts of the UK. That all requires an ongoing connection and immersion in information that is often considered too specialist and/or too niche to be considered relevant.

The psychology of relevance detection explores the cognitive mechanisms that enable humans to distinguish between relevant and irrelevant information. It seeks to understand how we filter out distractions, prioritise salient information, and make sense of the vast amount of data we encounter daily. According to relevance detection theory, our brains employ a dynamic interplay of top-down and bottom-up processes to determine relevance. Top-down processes, guided by our goals, expectations, and prior knowledge, shape our attention and guide our perception of what is relevant. Bottom-up processes, driven by the inherent salience of stimuli, capture our attention and draw our focus to novel, unexpected, or emotionally charged information.

The interplay of these top-down and bottom-up processes allows us to make rapid and efficient judgments about relevance. Our goals and expectations act as filters, guiding our attention to information that is likely to be relevant to our current task or interests. Simultaneously, salient stimuli can capture our attention even if they are not directly relevant to our goals, potentially alerting us to something important or unexpected. The ability to detect relevance is crucial for effective information processing and decision-making. It enables us to focus on the most pertinent information, filter out distractions, and avoid cognitive overload. This ability is essential for tasks ranging from everyday conversations and reading to complex problem-solving and scientific inquiry.

However, our ability to detect relevance is not infallible. Biases, heuristics, and cognitive limitations can influence our judgments, leading to errors in relevance assessment. For instance, confirmation bias can lead us to favour information that confirms our existing beliefs, while neglecting disconfirming evidence. Additionally, our limited attention span and working memory can make it challenging to process large amounts of information simultaneously, potentially leading to omissions of relevant details. Simply put, in order to decide if something is relevant or pertinent, we have to investigate and assess its criteria as well as applying our critical thinking to be able to do this. Let's take tracing to a more literal level given our subject matter here.

What is the point in telling you all that? There are words that I like to live by when working 'Everything is relevant, until it is not'. Now granted that is quite the cognitive load to bear and at times you can be at risk of taxing your cognitive capabilities as a result. This is why we go through the formative mindset training elements first and make sure that those responses are at the ground floor of your journey. So, tracing details of an individual we should be using any and all elements that are at our disposal in order to make sure we achieve the most effective outcome that is particular to our desired goal.

At the time of writing this particular paragraph, I am also reviewing my knowledge and awareness of different accents from around the world. Thanks in no small part to the variety of YouTube videos. One could make the argument that this is a complete waste of time and far too niche to be useful as it is easy to hear the difference between someone who is Irish and someone who is Australian, someone who is from Spain and someone who is from Wales. Yet there are those I have met; fully grown adults might I add, that can't hear the difference between the Scottish and Irish accents. If you were to listen to someone that said they are from Yorkshire, could you hear the difference between Leeds, Bradford, Huddersfield, York, Harrogate, Scarborough, Hull and Bridlington. I would wager unless you are from those areas then you would struggle. Yet depending on the presentation of information you have, this may be something that could aid your location of an individual immeasurably.

I ask this as well, who am I hurting in immersing myself in this knowledge too if I have the time to do it? Nobody. Therefore I feel no issue in advocating for its benefit due to having a grasp of most accents from around the world now. Thus immediately clueing me in to significant cultural influences on behaviour and building out the details from there based on just a small presentation of knowledge. After all:

"From a single drop of water, a logician should infer the possibility of an Atlantic or a Niagara without having seen or heard of one or the other."

In moving forwards then we will look at several means of profiling an individual and their acts based on a more criminal and asset location approach.

Top Down or Bottom Up

Imagine you're a detective investigating a crime scene. You have a hunch about who the culprit might be, so you start by gathering evidence that supports your hypothesis. This is essentially what top-down profiling is all about. It's an approach that starts with a general idea or theory and then works its way down to the specifics. The term "top-down" comes from the way we often think – from the general to the specific. For example, when you're planning a vacation, you might start by thinking about the overall destination and then gradually narrow down your choices to specific cities, hotels, and activities. Top-down profiling is often used in situations where there is a clear problem or goal to be addressed. For example, it is commonly used in business to identify potential customers, develop new products, or improve customer service.

The concept of top-down profiling is a field within offender profiling that came about in the 1970s, primarily through the work of the FBI's Behavioural Science Unit (BSU). The BSU, led by people like John Douglas, Robert Ressler, and Ann Burgess. They began to develop a systematic approach to understanding the characteristics and behaviours of serial criminals.

In their seminal work, "The Criminal Profile: A Study in Behavioural Science," Douglas and Ressler introduced the concept of "criminal typology," which suggested that serial offenders could be categorised into distinct types based on their shared personality traits, modus operandi, and victim selection. This approach formed the basis for top-down profiling, as it allowed investigators to develop hypotheses about the potential offender based on known characteristics of their crime.

Top-down profiling has also faced criticism for its subjectivity and reliance on generalisations about criminal behaviour. Critics have argued that the approach can lead to oversimplifications and misinterpretations, potentially narrowing the focus of investigations and overlooking alternative suspects. Despite these criticisms, top-down profiling remains a widely used technique in criminal investigations, particularly in cases involving serial or violent crimes. Investigators recognize that top-down profiling is not a definitive tool, but rather a starting point for generating hypotheses and guiding further investigations.

Bottom-up Profiling

Now, let's say you're a data scientist working for a company that sells online courses. You have access to a vast amount of data about your customers, such as their demographics, purchase history, and browsing behaviour. What do you do with all this data? This is where bottom-up profiling comes in. It's an approach that starts with the data and then works its way up to general insights or patterns. The term "bottom-up" comes from the way we often collect and analyse data – from the individual pieces to the broader picture.

For example, when you're studying for an exam, you might start by memorising individual facts and concepts. Then, you gradually connect these pieces to understand the bigger picture and develop a comprehensive understanding of the subject matter. Bottom-up profiling is often used in situations where there is no clear problem or goal to be addressed. Instead, the goal is to explore the data and discover hidden patterns or trends. For example, it is commonly used in scientific research to identify new genes or drugs, or in marketing to identify potential customers for new products.

The more astute amongst you will note that you are simply applying a different direction in reasoning based on the presentation of information that you have in conjunction with your purpose in being involved in the first place. If you are given data to form conclusions around, you are in bottom up territory and if it is the reverse then top down is the way that is before you. I would be remiss if I did not mention potential flaws that could arise in your early onset use of this in that one element should not neglect the other! They are akin to the likes of quantitative and qualitative research.

Quantitative and qualitative research are two broad approaches to conducting research that differ in their emphasis on data collection, analysis, and interpretation. Quantitative research focuses on collecting and analysing numerical data to quantify phenomena, identify patterns, and make generalisations about a population. It relies on structured methods, such as surveys, experiments, and statistical analysis, to collect data that can be quantified and numerically represented.

Qualitative research focuses on collecting and analysing non-numerical data, such as text, images, and audio recordings, to understand the meaning, experiences, and perspectives of individuals or groups. It utilises unstructured methods, such as interviews, observations, and content analysis, to collect data that captures rich details and nuances.

The concept of bottom-up profiling, which is somewhat ironically also known as inductive profiling, emerged in the 1980s as a counterpoint to the more established top-down profiling approach. Bottom-up profiling emphasises the analysis of specific case details to identify patterns and discern the unique characteristics of the offender. The development of bottom-up profiling is largely attributed to the work of British psychologist David Canter, who advocated for a data-driven approach that focused on the specific circumstances of each crime rather than relying on pre-existing offender categories. Canter's work emphasised the importance of analysing crime scene evidence, victim characteristics, and offender behaviour to develop a profile that was tailored to the specific case.

Bottom-up profiling gained traction in the 1990s as investigators recognized the limitations of top-down profiling and the need for a more nuanced approach that considered the unique aspects of each crime. Canter's work, along with the contributions of other researchers like Paul Britton and Lorraine Hope, helped establish bottom-up profiling as a valuable tool in criminal investigations.

The concepts of organised and disorganised offenders came out of the combination of both of these practices in a fashion. They differ in their methodologies, but they both contributed to the understanding of offender typologies and the identification of key characteristics that distinguish organised and disorganised criminals.

Top-down profiling's role in organised and disorganised offender typology

Top-down profiling, which relies on existing typologies and generalisations about criminal behaviour, played a significant role in establishing the distinction between organised and disorganised offenders. Roy Hazelwood and John Douglas began to identify patterns in the modus operandi and victim selection of serial criminals. They observed that certain offenders exhibited a high degree of planning, preparation, and control over their crimes, while others acted impulsively and left evidence of disorganisation at the crime scene.

Hazelwood and Douglas proposed a typology that categorised serial offenders into three main groups: organised, disorganised, and mixed. Organised offenders were characterised by their careful planning, meticulous attention to detail, and ability to control the crime scene and victim. Disorganised offenders, on the other hand, were characterised by their impulsive actions, lack of planning, and tendency to leave evidence behind.

Bottom-up profiling's contribution to understanding organised and disorganised offenders

Bottom-up profiling, with its focus on the specific details of each case, further refined the understanding of organised and disorganised offenders. By analysing crime scene evidence, victim characteristics, and offender behaviour, researchers like David Canter and Paul Britton identified specific patterns that distinguished these two types of offenders.

Canter proposed a framework that considered factors such as the offender's planning and preparation, their ability to control the crime scene and victim, their use of weapons, their post-offense behaviour, and their overall level of sophistication. Based on these factors, investigators could classify an offender as organised, disorganised, or mixed.

Organised offenders are typically characterised by the following traits: High degree of planning and preparation: They carefully plan their crimes, often conducting surveillance and gathering information about their victims.

Meticulous attention to detail: They take steps to conceal their identity, dispose of evidence effectively, and avoid leaving traces at the crime scene.

Ability to control the crime scene and victim: They subdue their victims efficiently, minimise time spent at the crime scene, and maintain control of the situation.

Social competence: They may have stable relationships, hold steady jobs, and appear normal in their daily lives.

Disorganised offenders, on the other hand, are typically characterised by the following traits: Impulsive actions: They act impulsively and without much planning, often committing crimes in a state of heightened emotion or arousal.

Lack of planning and preparation: They may not have a clear plan or motive, and they often make mistakes that leave evidence behind.

Inability to control the crime scene and victim: They may struggle to subdue their victims, leave a disorganised crime scene, and lack control over the situation.

Social difficulties: They may have a history of mental health issues, substance abuse, or social isolation.

Even with this rudimentary and somewhat basic profiling knowledge at hand, we can begin to use it in order to read the scenes and situations that people leave behind them. Take this for example:

The notion of criminals doesn't have to be on the table here but look at it simply through the lens of being organised or disorganised. What do the organised elements communicate to you? It is in the books no? The position of the chair? How about the disorganised things? The toys? Just the toys? Is this a lounge/Living room area or a separate area altogether?

Even doing it stringently - What are the impulsive signs to you or the elements that show a lack of preparation. I am creating the context for you as this is absolutely not a crime scene. Is there a 'control' over the scene or just certain parts? The answers you provide to these questions will aid in your ability to profile the individuals you are looking at, regardless of the situation you find them in.

Here is where I would like to draw a line of sorts as this is not a treatise on the ins and outs of criminal profiling. RAT profiling or the many disciplines of offender/geographic profiling are something I take great pride in working the ins and outs of, however there are far more superior books and textbooks on the topics than anything I could describe for you here. Should these be elements that you would like to make further use of then I would recommend taking some courses on them and immersing yourselves in the reading of such.

My intention in laying out the basics of top down/bottom up and the organised/disorganised elements is to show you the ways that these pieces of information can be transformed into something that you can work in any and all scenarios. Even though they come from criminal origins, the nature of being organised and/or disorganised is something that can and does appear in everyday life. The nature of information in this particular field of work is such that I would argue it might be close to Forest's box of chocolates in that you never quite know what you are going to get.

I am married to 'The work'

"I have no time for sentiment, Watson. I am a detective, and my work is my life." - "The Adventure of the Speckled Band"

I thought I would take this time to chat to you all about 'the work' namely the research and practice elements of all things involved in trying to develop these skills for yourself. I love that people take the time to ask questions about this and that or what I think about something pertaining to the work in this area. However there are a number of elements that I am asked so often that I have taken to making videos about them as well as blog posts and other communication forms. This then is an essay, a monograph if you will, in regards to the ways in which you can develop your palace of information and train certain elements yourself.

The work

This is something that cannot be understated. You have to work at these things, daily. I could cite a number of books to help you develop habitual qualities around this. James Clear's wonderful text Atomic Habits being at the top of the list but even then, when you look at something else as a way of doing work for you then you will not develop the habitual qualities that you need in order to make sure that you excel in the areas you would like. Whether it be this or any other area of interest that you have.

The discipline involved will go hand in hand with Cognitive load theory in that you will need to be aware of your capabilities with focus and your need for rest and recuperation. We are human after all, as much as some of us would like to pretend otherwise. This is a needed quality for making sure our cognition is as on point as it can be. Furthermore I am going to keep this part to just my thoughts and opinions where possible. It will be more along the lines of details on how I operate and not anything that I am advocating for or against one way or the other. Anyway (A friend of mine, Daniel, who has edited previous things I have written will be overjoyed to see I have not written any who. I like to write as I talk. Many advise against this but I want you to hear these words from my mouth and not some ai spellchecker or someone else) in order to get to grips with elements that this way of life contains, I would start with what could be considered as the basics and work my way out in to the niche areas from there.

These basics would be your memory skills, your state control, critical thinking, reasoning and your people reading, body language, NVC or whatever other term you want to use for looking at the movements of people in relation to the information it could communicate to you. A lot of people get really bent out of shape over the terminology in this area - people reading was one I was asked about as the complaint was that you can't read someone like a book really. No s***?! Personally I don't care what terminology is used so long as the application of material remains clear.

How do you do this you may wonder? Well this series of books should give you a great start but my recommendation beyond that is really not to discriminate. To get involved in anything and everything you can. Read, watch and listen to as much if not all that you can. This would be regardless of whether you know it to be rubbish or not and believe me there is A LOT of rubbish out there. Please don't be blinded by statements like 'I am number one in this' or 'I am a retired operative from' some 3 letter agency as that is just gimmick reliant and there is no real way of quantifying or even qualifying that nonsense. You can decide what is relevant to your life, work and practices. When I wanted to decide my views on religion, I read as many different texts as I could and looked for translations of the ones I couldn't read or understand. To cherry pick your information based on marketing effectiveness is lazy and will do you no favours at all. When I was watching the Neil deGrasse Tyson Masterclass on scientific thinking he spoke of analogy surrounding crystals.

Someone comes to you with a crystal and says, 'this is the best crystal ever and will cure diseases for you' were you to respond to this with 'Oh my god wow!' or 'Please leave me alone you idiot!' then both are just as intellectually lazy as the other and are governed by an opinion rather than a need to learn. If you responded by asking things like :

- How was this developed?
- What kind of diseases?
- Are there any settings requirements? Like heat or cold?
- Do I need anything else in conjunction with said crystal?
- How did you get it?
- Who else has it cured?

Then this avenue of thinking is demonstrative of your need to properly educate yourself on the way that you will interact with crystals moving forwards. You can apply the same thing here. So when people ask me what books I should read in order to develop, it is met by a dissonance of sorts in my head. On the one hand I am grateful for the question and your interest in my view but on the other, I am not even really sure what you mean. There are people that exist that I know write verifiable nonsense at times and yet I still read this in order to keep myself as educated in the realms of this world as possible so that I don't slip into it. So I advocate for reading, listening, watching and talking about everything you can within the timeframe you have available to do so.

There is a secondary and tertiary reason for this. You have no idea what is going to be relevant to your work tomorrow. It could involve dogs, foot cream, earrings, tattoos ANYTHING. How are you going to be as effective in your role as a Deductionist if you have to say I am sorry, let me just google what that is. Now don't get me wrong, you can't know everything. It is the predisposition towards determining if something is effective or not before you even really know what it is. In that vein, you would be as bad as someone who reviews something on Amazon without even making the verified purchase of it. There was a time a few years ago when I was reading about the different kinds of tears and the effects they can have on the skin under the eyes. I don't need to detail the workings of that here for you but it would be obvious enough to say that this is some niche information for sure. The first time I used that piece of information in a work setting was not until years after. Do you have to go that far? Not unless you want to, no, what I would encourage you to do on the back of this would be to not literally judge a book by its cover. Read it and above all, use it. If it isn't something you end up using on a day to day basis and there are other pieces of information jostling for room in your palace then make the call to remove one element in favour of the other. In approaching the development of your knowledge in this way, you will have to, by default, keep an open and non-judgmental mind about things and not fall foul of any critically reasoned flaws because of a misalignment in your states.

The tertiary reason would be your presence. This is most often attributed to mindfulness. At this stage, I have yet to read something on the topic of mindfulness that didn't boil down to simply 'be more mindful'. Leaving me wondering 'Ok, how??" The research on the benefits in this area remains clear. Mitigating the negative effects of stress and anxiety and enhancing cognitive capability. If you have no reactionary judgement or bias presentation when you are listening to a podcast or taking an online course, then by default you are more engaged with the information and are listening, or at the very least, attempting to listen to the information for exactly what it is and not how you perceive it to be. Much like the research on self-talk and cognitive capability, we are just listening to information before it gets coloured in a wash of emotion. That is such a beneficial skill for the modern day deductionist.

Skill Transfer

I am going to preface this story by saying that the guy in question now knows better and was very much in the 'not being able to see the wood for the trees category' in regards to memory. We had gone over a few techniques and I was showing him how it is possible to profile people at the poker table by remembering details. He had done 25 individual details in a couple of minutes which is pretty good going for a first session and these weren't even short one word details. His comment on our third session was words to the effect of 'I can remember more, so what?'

Dissonance abounds in my head. Massively!!

On the one hand, I more than most, appreciate raw honesty when it isn't some vain attempt to be insulting. It is just saying what you are thinking. So few people are capable of doing that. On the other hand I am thinking 'what do you even mean?!" You now function more effectively than 90% (a made up stat based on my feelings as I can't review this bit) of the people around you and you outperform pretty much all of the general public if you listen to anything Miller and Ebbinghaus have done within the field of Memory research. The more we talked the more I understood that he didn't understand at that time just how transferable a memory skill was.

Naturally I am now curious as to the other areas of skill that this thought process may affect, and so, here we are.

When you think of what it would take to memorise a shopping list or heaven forbid, even a pack of cards, what are you thinking about? What is that skill to you? Is it just the single serving entity of some cute skill or trait? Or is it something else? I would hope for the latter as opposed to the former. No matter the thing you are using in the earlier stages of your training it should be enough to indicate to you that you have the capacity for more. I would like to stop a potential train of thought here before it goes any further. This is not mentioned to be anything akin to something 'self-help' esque, more my small attempts to show you the differing ways that something can be used.

You can memorise a deck of cards in a couple of minutes, awesome. That does not mean that, that is all that you can do. 52 of these things would show you that you can do 52 anything. Maybe not straight away but if you have the capacity for 52 cards then you have the capacity for 52 anything. 52 facts about someone you are observing, 52 street names and directions in your local area, 52 random thoughts that your partner has and says out loud over the course of that week. 52 songs your children tell you that they like. There is no doubt that the systems that you use would have to be tweaked and changed along the way. Just the way in which you approach these different aspects will, I hope, show you your own capacity for making your life infinitely easier. If you are a little like Alexander. Not in his approach to life, as from what I read, he wasn't a very nice man. Being more akin to his moniker is something that you will be able to make perfect use of. Being 'the man who knows' or the woman who knows or anything else. 'Knowing' is what I am getting at. The more you can store in your head the easier everything else will become as a result.

Not an advocacy speech for the powers of memory training though I could wax lyrical about that for hours on end. If anything what I am advocating for is investing your time and focus into yourselves and less into the technological endeavours we surround ourselves with. Give yourselves a little more credit for being the wonderful concoctions of electricity and grey matter you are. Some choose to do nothing with that or even terrible things, but you, you know differently now.

How do I......

Again this is something that I am to be involved in multiple times throughout the course of a day. It is a catch 22 in the face of the fact that I really and genuinely appreciate that there are those out there that genuinely appreciate my answers or find some value in what I say. That is a humbling and lovely sentiment. The other side of me thinks that my response lets them down slightly. It is simply because my answer is an easy one, for pretty much all of the variations of this very idea.

I will give you an idea as to some of the variations I get:
- How do I develop a better memory?
- How do I deduce quickly?
- How do I read people accurately?
- How do I develop a memory palace?

The questions may change but the start of them always remains the same. As do my answers. Use it! To illustrate it more directly:

- How do I develop a better memory? Use it
- How do I deduce quickly? By Deducing
- How do I read people accurately? By trying to read people
- How do I develop a memory palace? By building one

It struck me that there are many different reasons for asking the questions and it might be because you feel you don't know, or you can't or something else. There are no shortcuts, there is no fast track. I am going to type the next thought in capital letters in the hope that it comes across as clear as is humanly possible. THIS WILL TAKE A LOT OF TIME AND EFFORT TO DEVELOP FOR YOURSELF. The fact of the matter remains that there is no magic trick to this, if you want to test your memory in a 'Sherlockian' sort of way then it would be very apparent how to do that after some thought. The next stage would be to, you know, do it. I would wager that if there were any questions about any skill development of any kind, that exist in your head at this moment. They could be solved by doing it. Following a brief stint of ingesting knowledge of course and is why you have read this book. After that:

- If you want to learn a language, speak it.
- If you want to be a chef. Cook.
- If you want to learn an instrument. Play it.
- If you want to be in a relationship. Be in one.
- If you want to run a business. Start one.

The list goes on and on and on. The intention with the closing part of the first book was to show you how many different people could use these skills. If you are reading this then you already have an understanding that anyone from anywhere can benefit from developing this way of looking at the world.

My intention in closing the book this time is for you to actually go and start using it. Go and apply. Not that it wasn't before but it is even more so now. Stop this from being something quirky you read one time about how someone created a skillset from someone fictional and just go and do it. Use it! I want this skillset to be broken. As in, if there is someone out there that can show me that something I am working on is b******t or can be changed by doing something else then I want to know about it. The only way I can do that right now is for as many different people in as many different situations as is possible to be trying and testing this. I have no ego about any of it. I have developed and worked on all of this in the ways that I know how to do. After all of that, I don't know what I don't know right? So let's develop this together from here on! Let's put our heads together on something that will help you to level up anything and everything you do!

As far as my research goes, these next words can be traced back to one man. For those of us alive in 2023 we won't know if he said them for sure or not but the sentiment of the sentence remains regardless.

"Observe carefully and deduce shrewdly."

Be thorough, be careful, be relentless in your approach to success with this. Be shrewd, be critical and be exploratory in how you find and assess the information you work with. These words were uttered by Joseph Bell. This man was the real life inspiration behind the best and wisest man whom I have ever known. Sherlock Holmes. In this next chapter I sincerely hope that that person, is you.

Bibliography

Abe, M., & Hanakawa, T. (2009). Functional coupling underlying motor and cognitive functions of the dorsal premotor cortex. Behavioural Brain Research, 198(1), 13–23. https://doi.org/10.1016/j.bbr.2008.10.046

Boly, M., Phillips, C., Tshibanda, L., Vanhaudenhuyse, A., Schabus, M., Dang-Vu, T. T., Moonen, G., Hustinx, R., Maquet, P., & Laureys, S. (2008). Intrinsic Brain Activity in Altered States of Consciousness: How Conscious Is the Default Mode of Brain Function? Annals of the New York Academy of Sciences, 1129(1), 119–129. https://doi.org/10.1196/annals.1417.015

Chance, B., Zhuang, Z., UnAh, C., Alter, C., & Lipton, L. (1993). Cognition-activated low-frequency modulation of light absorption in human brain. Proceedings of the National Academy of Sciences, 90(8), 3770–3774. https://doi.org/10.1073/pnas.90.8.3770

Costa, J., Adams, A. T., Jung, M. F., Guimbretière, F., & Choudhury, T. (2016). EmotionCheck: Leveraging bodily signals and false feedback to regulate our emotions. Proceedings of the 2016 ACM International Joint Conference on Pervasive and Ubiquitous Computing, 758–769. https://doi.org/10.1145/2971648.2971752

Daram, A., Yanguas-Gil, A., & Kudithipudi, D. (2020). Exploring Neuromodulation for Dynamic Learning. Frontiers in Neuroscience, 14, 928. https://doi.org/10.3389/fnins.2020.00928

Gray, J. R. (2004). Integration of Emotion and Cognitive Control. Current Directions in Psychological Science, 13(2), 46–48. https://doi.org/10.1111/j.0963-7214.2004.00272.x

Hannawi, Y., Lindquist, M. A., Caffo, B. S., Sair, H. I., & Stevens, R. D. (2015). Resting brain activity in disorders of consciousness: A systematic review and meta-analysis. Neurology, 84(12), 1272–1280. https://doi.org/10.1212/WNL.0000000000001404

Inzlicht, M., Bartholow, B. D., & Hirsh, J. B. (2015). Emotional foundations of cognitive control. Trends in Cognitive Sciences, 19(3), 126–132. https://doi.org/10.1016/j.tics.2015.01.004

Javaheripour, N., Shahdipour, N., Noori, K., Zarei, M., Camilleri, J. A., Laird, A. R., Fox, P. T., Eickhoff, S. B., Eickhoff, C. R., Rosenzweig, I., Khazaie, H., & Tahmasian, M. (2019). Functional brain alterations in acute sleep deprivation: An activation likelihood estimation meta-analysis. Sleep Medicine Reviews, 46, 64–73. https://doi.org/10.1016/j.smrv.2019.03.008

Katona, J., Farkas, I., Ujbanyi, T., Dukan, P., & Kovari, A. (2014). Evaluation of the NeuroSky MindFlex EEG headset brain waves data. 2014 IEEE 12th International Symposium on Applied Machine Intelligence and Informatics (SAMI), 91–94. https://doi.org/10.1109/SAMI.2014.6822382

Mantini, D., Gerits, A., Nelissen, K., Durand, J.-B., Joly, O., Simone, L., Sawamura, H., Wardak, C., Orban, G. A., Buckner, R. L., &

Vanduffel, W. (2011). Default Mode of Brain Function in Monkeys. The Journal of Neuroscience, 31(36), 12954–12962. https://doi.org/10.1523/JNEUROSCI.2318-11.2011

Maquet, P., Ruby, P., Maudoux, A., Albouy, G., Sterpenich, V., Dang-Vu, T., Desseilles, M., Boly, M., Perrin, F., Peigneux, P., & Laureys, S. (2005). Human cognition during REM sleep and the activity profile within frontal and parietal cortices: A reappraisal of functional neuroimaging data. In Progress in Brain Research (Vol. 150, pp. 219–595). Elsevier. https://doi.org/10.1016/S0079-6123(05)50016-5

McCormick, D. A., Nestvogel, D. B., & He, B. J. (2020). Neuromodulation of Brain State and Behavior. Annual Review of Neuroscience, 43(1), 391–415. https://doi.org/10.1146/annurev-neuro-100219-105424

McRae, K. (2016). Cognitive emotion regulation: A review of theory and scientific findings. Current Opinion in Behavioral Sciences, 10, 119–124. https://doi.org/10.1016/j.cobeha.2016.06.004

Moussa, M. N., Vechlekar, C. D., Burdette, J. H., Steen, M. R., Hugenschmidt, C. E., & Laurienti, P. J. (2011). Changes in Cognitive State Alter Human Functional Brain Networks. Frontiers in Human Neuroscience, 5. https://doi.org/10.3389/fnhum.2011.00083

Muller, A. M., & Meyer, M. (2014). Language in the brain at rest: New insights from resting state data and graph theoretical analysis.

Frontiers in Human Neuroscience, 8. https://doi.org/10.3389/fnhum.2014.00228

Ochsner, K., & Gross, J. (2005). The cognitive control of emotion. Trends in Cognitive Sciences, 9(5), 242–249. https://doi.org/10.1016/j.tics.2005.03.010

Roohi-Azizi, M., Azimi, L., Heysieattalab, S., & Aamidfar, M. (2017). Changes of the brain's bioelectrical activity in cognition, consciousness, and some mental disorders. Medical Journal of the Islamic Republic of Iran, 31(1), 307–312. https://doi.org/10.14196/mjiri.31.53

Sagi, Y., Tavor, I., Hofstetter, S., Tzur-Moryosef, S., Blumenfeld-Katzir, T., & Assaf, Y. (2012). Learning in the Fast Lane: New Insights into Neuroplasticity. Neuron, 73(6), 1195–1203. https://doi.org/10.1016/j.neuron.2012.01.025

Schmidgall, S., & Hays, J. (2022). Learning to learn online with neuromodulated synaptic plasticity in spiking neural networks [Preprint]. Neuroscience. https://doi.org/10.1101/2022.06.24.497562

Tansey, M. A. (1985). Brainwave signatures — An index reflective of the brain's functional neuroanatomy: Further findings on the effect of EEG sensorimotor rhythm biofeedback training on the neurologic precursors of learning disabilities. International Journal of Psychophysiology, 3(2), 85–99. https://doi.org/10.1016/0167-8760(85)90030-3

Wang, P., Kong, R., Kong, X., Liégeois, R., Orban, C., Deco, G., Van Den Heuvel, M. P., & Thomas Yeo, B. T. (2019). Inversion of a large-scale circuit model reveals a cortical hierarchy in the dynamic resting human brain. Science Advances, 5(1), eaat7854. https://doi.org/10.1126/sciadv.aat7854

Yasui, Y. (2009). A Brainwave Signal Measurement and Data Processing Technique for Daily Life Applications. Journal of PHYSIOLOGICAL ANTHROPOLOGY, 28(3), 145–150. https://doi.org/10.2114/jpa2.28.145

Ziegler, U. M., Hawkes, L. W., & Lacher, R. C. (1992). Rapid learning with large weight changes and plasticity. [Proceedings 1992] IJCNN International Joint Conference on Neural Networks, 2, 146–151. https://doi.org/10.1109/IJCNN.1992.227016

Beatty, E. L., & Vartanian, O. (2015). The prospects of working memory training for improving deductive reasoning. Frontiers in Human Neuroscience, 9. https://doi.org/10.3389/fnhum.2015.00056

Bhagavatula, C., Bras, R. L., Malaviya, C., Sakaguchi, K., Holtzman, A., Rashkin, H., Downey, D., Yih, S. W., & Choi, Y. (2020). Abductive Commonsense Reasoning (arXiv:1908.05739). arXiv. http://arxiv.org/abs/1908.05739

Coscia, L., Causa, P., Giuliani, E., & Nunziata, A. (1975). Pharmacological properties of new neuroleptic compounds. Arzneimittel-Forschung, 25(9), 1436–1442.

Csikszentmihalyi, M., & Halton, E. (1981). The meaning of things: Domestic symbols and the self. Cambridge University Press.

Dwyer, C. P., Hogan, M. J., & Stewart, I. (2014). An integrated critical thinking framework for the 21st century. Thinking Skills and Creativity, 12, 43–52. https://doi.org/10.1016/j.tsc.2013.12.004

Ennis, R. H. (1993). Critical thinking assessment. Theory Into Practice, 32(3), 179–186. https://doi.org/10.1080/00405849309543594

Folger, R., & Stein, C. (2017). Abduction 101: Reasoning processes to aid discovery. Human Resource Management Review, 27(2), 306–315. https://doi.org/10.1016/j.hrmr.2016.08.007

Folks, J. L. (2005). P eirce, C harles S anders. In P. Armitage & T. Colton (Eds.), Encyclopedia of Biostatistics (1st ed.). Wiley. https://doi.org/10.1002/0470011815.b2a17115

García-Madruga, J. A., Orenes, I., Vila Chaves, J. Ó., & Gómez-Veiga, I. (2022). Executive Functions and Improvement of Thinking: An Intervention Program to Enhance Deductive Reasoning Abilities. The Spanish Journal of Psychology, 25, e32. https://doi.org/10.1017/SJP.2022.26

Gill, J. H., & Bernstein, R. J. (1967). Perspectives on Peirce: Critical Essays on Charles Saunders Peirce. Philosophy and

Phenomenological Research, 27(3), 458. https://doi.org/10.2307/2106088

Goel, Ramanujam, & Sadayappan. (1988). Towards a 'neural' architecture for abductive reasoning. IEEE International Conference on Neural Networks, 681–688 vol.1. https://doi.org/10.1109/ICNN.1988.23906

Halpern, D. F. (1998). Teaching critical thinking for transfer across domains: Disposition, skills, structure training, and metacognitive monitoring. American Psychologist, 53(4), 449–455. https://doi.org/10.1037/0003-066X.53.4.449

Hayes, B. K., & Heit, E. (2018). Inductive reasoning 2.0. WIREs Cognitive Science, 9(3), e1459. https://doi.org/10.1002/wcs.1459

Hoch, S. J., & Tschirgi, J. E. (1985). Logical knowledge and cue redundancy in deductive reasoning. Memory & Cognition, 13(5), 453–462. https://doi.org/10.3758/BF03198458

Ketokivi, M., & Mantere, S. (2010). Two Strategies for Inductive Reasoning in Organizational Research. Academy of Management Review, 35(2), 315–333. https://doi.org/10.5465/amr.35.2.zok315

Klauer, K. J., & Phye, G. D. (2008). Inductive Reasoning: A Training Approach. Review of Educational Research, 78(1), 85–123. https://doi.org/10.3102/0034654307313402

237

Kulik, A. M., & Kondrat'eva, L. N. (1975). [Combined effects of hypoxia and hypercapnia on the functional state of the respiratory center]. Biulleten' Eksperimental'noi Biologii I Meditsiny, 79(4), 39–43.

Leighton, J. P. (2006). Teaching and Assessing Deductive Reasoning Skills. The Journal of Experimental Education, 74(2), 107–136. https://doi.org/10.3200/JEXE.74.2.107-136

Li, D., & Cellier, F. E. (1990). Fuzzy measures in inductive reasoning. 1990 Winter Simulation Conference Proceedings, 527–538. https://doi.org/10.1109/WSC.1990.129571

Markovits, H., Schleifer, M., & Fortier, L. (1989). Development of elementary deductive reasoning in young children. Developmental Psychology, 25(5), 787–793. https://doi.org/10.1037/0012-1649.25.5.787

Mirza, N. A., Akhtar-Danesh, N., Noesgaard, C., Martin, L., & Staples, E. (2014). A concept analysis of abductive reasoning. Journal of Advanced Nursing, 70(9), 1980–1994. https://doi.org/10.1111/jan.12379

Oaksford, M. (2015). Imaging deductive reasoning and the new paradigm. Frontiers in Human Neuroscience, 9. https://doi.org/10.3389/fnhum.2015.00101

Park, J., & Lee, K.-H. (2018). Introduction to the Special Issue on Abductive Reasoning in Mathematics Education. EURASIA Journal of Mathematics, Science and Technology Education, 14(9). https://doi.org/10.29333/ejmste/92551

Pearce, S. M. (Ed.). (1994). Interpreting objects and collections. Routledge.

Prado, J., Chadha, A., & Booth, J. R. (2011). The Brain Network for Deductive Reasoning: A Quantitative Meta-analysis of 28 Neuroimaging Studies. Journal of Cognitive Neuroscience, 23(11), 3483–3497. https://doi.org/10.1162/jocn_a_00063

Stephens, R. G., Dunn, J. C., Hayes, B., & Kalish, M. (2020). A test of two processes: The effect of training on deductive and inductive reasoning [Preprint]. PsyArXiv. https://doi.org/10.31234/osf.io/bx3tj
The Rule of reason: The philosophy of Charles Sanders Peirce. (1997). Choice Reviews Online, 35(01), 35-0220-35–0220. https://doi.org/10.5860/CHOICE.35-0220

Tóth, P., & Pogatsnik, M. (2023). Advancement of inductive reasoning of engineering students. Hungarian Educational Research Journal, 13(1), 86–106. https://doi.org/10.1556/063.2022.00120
Van Vo, D., & Csapó, B. (2020). Development of inductive reasoning in students across school grade levels. Thinking Skills and Creativity, 37, 100699. https://doi.org/10.1016/j.tsc.2020.100699

Wang, L., Zhang, M., Zou, F., Wu, X., & Wang, Y. (2020). Deductive-reasoning brain networks: A coordinate-based meta-analysis of the neural signatures in deductive reasoning. Brain and Behavior, 10(12), e01853. https://doi.org/10.1002/brb3.1853

Wells, K. (2009). Learning and Teaching Critical Thinking: From a Peircean Perspective. Educational Philosophy and Theory, 41(2), 201–218. https://doi.org/10.1111/j.1469-5812.2007.00376.x

Wendelken, C. (2015). Meta-analysis: How does posterior parietal cortex contribute to reasoning? Frontiers in Human Neuroscience, 8. https://doi.org/10.3389/fnhum.2014.01042

Abdullah Batobara, M., & Sayed, A. A. (2020). Sherlock Holmes' Ability of the Mind and its Timeless Appeal. Scholars International Journal of Linguistics and Literature, 03(05), 164–170. https://doi.org/10.36348/sijll.2020.v03i05.005

André, D., & Fernand, G. (2008). Sherlock Holmes – an expert's view of expertise. British Journal of Psychology, 99(1), 109–125. https://doi.org/10.1348/000712607X224469

Ayers, M. S., & Reder, L. M. (1998). A theoretical review of the misinformation effect: Predictions from an activation-based memory model. Psychonomic Bulletin & Review, 5(1), 1–21. https://doi.org/10.3758/BF03209454

Bandura, A. (1989). Regulation of cognitive processes through perceived self-efficacy. Developmental Psychology, 25(5), 729–735. https://doi.org/10.1037/0012-1649.25.5.729

Barral, S., Cosentino, S., Christensen, K., Newman, A. B., Perls, T. T., Province, M. A., & Mayeux, R. (2014). Common Genetic Variants on 6q24 Associated With Exceptional Episodic Memory Performance in the Elderly. JAMA Neurology, 71(12), 1514. https://doi.org/10.1001/jamaneurol.2014.1663

Calev, A. (1996). Affect Memory in Depression: Evidence of Better Delayed Recall of Positive than Negative Affect Words. Psychopathology, 29(2), 71–76. https://doi.org/10.1159/000284974

Chow, Y. W., Pietranico, R., & Mukerji, A. (1975). Studies of oxygen binding energy to hemoglobin molecule. Biochemical and Biophysical Research Communications, 66(4), 1424–1431. https://doi.org/10.1016/0006-291x(75)90518-5

Drinkwater, B. A. (1976). Visual memory skills of medium contact aboriginal children. Australian Journal of Psychology, 28(1), 37–43. https://doi.org/10.1080/00049537608255261

Frank, G. (2004). Memory and Gender in Medieval Europe, 900–1200. By Elisabeth van Houts. Toronto: University of Toronto Press, 1999. xii + 196 pp. $50.00 cloth; Church History, 73(1), 199–200. https://doi.org/10.1017/S0009640700097912

Garry, M., & Hayne, H. (Eds.). (2013). Do Justice and Let the Sky Fall (0 ed.). Psychology Press. https://doi.org/10.4324/9780203774861

George, A. (2013). Elizabeth Loftus: The false memories that pervade our lives could have therapeutic uses. New Scientist, 219(2931), 28–29. https://doi.org/10.1016/S0262-4079(13)62090-4

Grilli, M. D., & Glisky, E. L. (2013). Imagining a Better Memory: Self-Imagination in Memory-Impaired Patients. Clinical Psychological Science, 1(1), 93–99. https://doi.org/10.1177/2167702612456464

Johnson, H. M., & Seifert, C. M. (1994). Sources of the continued influence effect: When misinformation in memory affects later inferences. Journal of Experimental Psychology: Learning, Memory, and Cognition, 20(6), 1420–1436. https://doi.org/10.1037/0278-7393.20.6.1420

Jones, W. E., Benge, J. F., & Scullin, M. K. (2021). Preserving prospective memory in daily life: A systematic review and meta-analysis of mnemonic strategy, cognitive training, external memory aid, and combination interventions. Neuropsychology, 35(1), 123–140. https://doi.org/10.1037/neu0000704

Kearney, A. (2012). Present Memories: Indigenous Memory Construct and Cross-Generational Knowledge Exchange in Northern Australia. In E. Keightley (Ed.), Time, Media and Modernity (pp. 165–183). Palgrave Macmillan UK. https://doi.org/10.1057/9781137020680_9

Kelly, L. (2015). Knowledge and power in prehistoric societies: Orality, memory, and the transmission of culture. Cambridge University Press.

Kelly, L. (2017a). The memory code. Simon and Schuster.

Kelly, L. (2017b). The memory code: Unlocking the secrets of the lives of the ancients and the power of the human mind. Atlantic Books.

Kelly, L., & Gojak, D. (2016). The Memory Code: The traditional Aboriginal memory technique that unlocks the secrets of Stonehenge, Easter Island and ancient monuments the world over. Volume Forty 2016, 40, 333.

Kelly, L., Keaten, J. A., & Finch, C. (2004). Reticent and non-reticent college students' preferred communication channels for interacting with faculty. Communication Research Reports, 21(2), 197–209.

Kim, J., Kwon, J. H., Kim, J., Kim, E. J., Kim, H. E., Kyeong, S., & Kim, J.-J. (2021). The effects of positive or negative self-talk on the alteration of brain functional connectivity by performing cognitive tasks. Scientific Reports, 11(1), 14873. https://doi.org/10.1038/s41598-021-94328-9

Lejbak, L., Vrbancic, M., & Crossley, M. (2009). The female advantage in object location memory is robust to verbalizability and mode of presentation of test stimuli. Brain and Cognition, 69(1), 148–153. https://doi.org/10.1016/j.bandc.2008.06.006

Levy, B. (1996). Improving memory in old age through implicit self-stereotyping. Journal of Personality and Social Psychology, 71(6), 1092–1107. https://doi.org/10.1037/0022-3514.71.6.1092

Long, S. (2017). Excavating the Memory Palace: An Account of the Disappearance of Mnemonic Imagery from English Rhetoric 1550–1650. Rhetoric Review, 36(2), 122–138. https://doi.org/10.1080/07350198.2017.1281691

McLaughlin, D. (2016). The Game's Afoot: Walking as Practice in Sherlockian Literary Geographies. https://doi.org/10.17863/CAM.9474

Memory and Gender in Medieval Europe, 900-1200. Elisabeth van Houts. (2001). Speculum, 76(1), 242–243. https://doi.org/10.2307/2903777

Newbury, C. (2019). The role of sleep in memory consolidation: Effects of lateralisation and emotion [Application/pdf]. 6713177 B, 342 pages. https://doi.org/10.17635/LANCASTER/THESIS/584

Reser, D., Simmons, M., Johns, E., Ghaly, A., Quayle, M., Dordevic, A. L., Tare, M., McArdle, A., Willems, J., & Yunkaporta, T. (2021). Australian Aboriginal techniques for memorization: Translation into a medical and allied health education setting. PLOS ONE, 16(5), e0251710. https://doi.org/10.1371/journal.pone.0251710

Sanner, T. (1975). Formation of transient complexes in the glutamate dehydrogenase catalyzed reaction. Biochemistry, 14(23), 5094–5098. https://doi.org/10.1021/bi00694a011

Scoboria, A., Wade, K. A., Lindsay, D. S., Azad, T., Strange, D., Ost, J., & Hyman, I. E. (2017). A mega-analysis of memory reports from eight peer-reviewed false memory implantation studies. Memory, 25(2), 146–163. https://doi.org/10.1080/09658211.2016.1260747

Severi, C. (2012). The arts of memory: Comparative perspectives on a mental artifact. HAU: Journal of Ethnographic Theory, 2(2), 451–485. https://doi.org/10.14318/hau2.2.025

Speer, M. E., & Delgado, M. R. (2017). Reminiscing about positive memories buffers acute stress responses. Nature Human Behaviour, 1(5), 0093. https://doi.org/10.1038/s41562-017-0093

Stephan, Y., Sutin, A. R., Luchetti, M., & Terracciano, A. (2020). Personality and memory performance over twenty years: Findings from three prospective studies. Journal of Psychosomatic Research, 128, 109885. https://doi.org/10.1016/j.jpsychores.2019.109885

Stopa, L., & Jenkins, A. (2007). Images of the self in social anxiety: Effects on the retrieval of autobiographical memories. Journal of Behavior Therapy and Experimental Psychiatry, 38(4), 459–473. https://doi.org/10.1016/j.jbtep.2007.08.006

Viard, A., Desgranges, B., Eustache, F., & Piolino, P. (2012). Factors affecting medial temporal lobe engagement for past and future episodic events: An ALE meta-analysis of neuroimaging studies. Brain and Cognition, 80(1), 111–125. https://doi.org/10.1016/j.bandc.2012.05.004

Witkowski, T. (2020). Elizabeth F. Loftus: Cognitive Psychology, Witness Testimony and Human Memory. In T. Witkowski, Shaping Psychology (pp. 11–27). Springer International Publishing. https://doi.org/10.1007/978-3-030-50003-0_2

Abdullah Batobara, M., & Sayed, A. A. (2020). Sherlock Holmes' Ability of the Mind and its Timeless Appeal. Scholars International Journal of Linguistics and Literature, 03(05), 164–170. https://doi.org/10.36348/sijll.2020.v03i05.005

André, D., & Fernand, G. (2008). Sherlock Holmes – an expert's view of expertise. British Journal of Psychology, 99(1), 109–125. https://doi.org/10.1348/000712607X224469

Ayers, M. S., & Reder, L. M. (1998). A theoretical review of the misinformation effect: Predictions from an activation-based memory model.
Psychonomic Bulletin & Review, 5(1), 1–21. https://doi.org/10.3758/BF03209454

Bandura, A. (1989). Regulation of cognitive processes through perceived self-efficacy. Developmental Psychology, 25(5), 729–735. https://doi.org/10.1037/0012-1649.25.5.729

Barral, S., Cosentino, S., Christensen, K., Newman, A. B., Perls, T. T., Province, M. A., & Mayeux, R. (2014). Common Genetic Variants on 6q24 Associated With Exceptional Episodic Memory Performance in the Elderly. JAMA Neurology, 71(12), 1514. https://doi.org/10.1001/jamaneurol.2014.1663

Calev, A. (1996). Affect Memory in Depression: Evidence of Better Delayed Recall of Positive than Negative Affect Words. Psychopathology, 29(2), 71–76. https://doi.org/10.1159/000284974

Chow, Y. W., Pietranico, R., & Mukerji, A. (1975). Studies of oxygen binding energy to hemoglobin molecule. Biochemical and Biophysical Research Communications, 66(4), 1424–1431. https://doi.org/10.1016/0006-291x(75)90518-5

Drinkwater, B. A. (1976). Visual memory skills of medium contact aboriginal children. Australian Journal of Psychology, 28(1), 37–43. https://doi.org/10.1080/00049537608255261

Frank, G. (2004). Memory and Gender in Medieval Europe, 900–1200. By Elisabeth van Houts. Toronto: University of Toronto Press, 1999. https://doi.org/10.1017/S0009640700097912

Garry, M., & Hayne, H. (Eds.). (2013). Do Justice and Let the Sky Fall (0 ed.). Psychology Press. https://doi.org/10.4324/9780203774861

George, A. (2013). Elizabeth Loftus: The false memories that pervade our lives could have therapeutic uses. New Scientist, 219(2931), 28–29. https://doi.org/10.1016/S0262-4079(13)62090-4

Grilli, M. D., & Glisky, E. L. (2013). Imagining a Better Memory: Self-Imagination in Memory-Impaired Patients. Clinical Psychological Science, 1(1), 93–99. https://doi.org/10.1177/2167702612456464

Johnson, H. M., & Seifert, C. M. (1994). Sources of the continued influence effect: When misinformation in memory affects later inferences. Journal of Experimental Psychology: Learning, Memory, and Cognition, 20(6), 1420–1436. https://doi.org/10.1037/0278-7393.20.6.1420

Jones, W. E., Benge, J. F., & Scullin, M. K. (2021). Preserving prospective memory in daily life: A systematic review and meta-analysis of mnemonic strategy, cognitive training, external memory aid, and combination interventions. Neuropsychology, 35(1), 123–140. https://doi.org/10.1037/neu0000704

Kearney, A. (2012). Present Memories: Indigenous Memory Construct and Cross-Generational Knowledge Exchange in Northern Australia. In E. Keightley (Ed.), Time, Media and Modernity (pp. 165–183). Palgrave Macmillan UK. https://doi.org/10.1057/9781137020680_9

Kelly, L. (2015). Knowledge and power in prehistoric societies: Orality, memory, and the transmission of culture. Cambridge University Press.

Kelly, L. (2017a). The memory code. Simon and Schuster.

Kelly, L. (2017b). The memory code: Unlocking the secrets of the lives of the ancients and the power of the human mind. Atlantic Books.

Kelly, L., & Gojak, D. (2016). The Memory Code: The traditional Aboriginal memory technique that unlocks the secrets of Stonehenge, Easter Island and ancient monuments the world over. Volume Forty 2016, 40, 333.

Kelly, L., Keaten, J. A., & Finch, C. (2004). Reticent and non-reticent college students' preferred communication channels for interacting with faculty. Communication Research Reports, 21(2), 197–209.

Kim, J., Kwon, J. H., Kim, J., Kim, E. J., Kim, H. E., Kyeong, S., & Kim, J.-J. (2021). The effects of positive or negative self-talk on the alteration of brain functional connectivity by performing cognitive tasks. Scientific Reports, 11(1), 14873. https://doi.org/10.1038/s41598-021-94328-9

Lejbak, L., Vrbancic, M., & Crossley, M. (2009). The female advantage in object location memory is robust to verbalizability and mode of presentation of test stimuli. Brain and Cognition, 69(1), 148–153. https://doi.org/10.1016/j.bandc.2008.06.006

Levy, B. (1996). Improving memory in old age through implicit self-stereotyping. Journal of Personality and Social Psychology, 71(6), 1092–1107. https://doi.org/10.1037/0022-3514.71.6.1092

Long, S. (2017). Excavating the Memory Palace: An Account of the Disappearance of Mnemonic Imagery from English Rhetoric 1550–1650. Rhetoric Review, 36(2), 122–138. https://doi.org/10.1080/07350198.2017.1281691

McLaughlin, D. (2016). The Game's Afoot: Walking as Practice in Sherlockian Literary Geographies. https://doi.org/10.17863/CAM.9474

Memory and Gender in Medieval Europe, 900-1200. Elisabeth van Houts. (2001). Speculum, 76(1), 242–243. https://doi.org/10.2307/2903777

Newbury, C. (2019). The role of sleep in memory consolidation: Effects of lateralisation and emotion [Application/pdf]. 6713177 B, 342 pages. https://doi.org/10.17635/LANCASTER/THESIS/584

Reser, D., Simmons, M., Johns, E., Ghaly, A., Quayle, M., Dordevic, A. L., Tare, M., McArdle, A., Willems, J., & Yunkaporta, T. (2021). Australian Aboriginal techniques for memorization: Translation into a medical and allied health education setting. PLOS ONE, 16(5), e0251710. https://doi.org/10.1371/journal.pone.0251710

Scoboria, A., Wade, K. A., Lindsay, D. S., Azad, T., Strange, D., Ost, J., & Hyman, I. E. (2017). A mega-analysis of memory reports from eight peer-reviewed false memory implantation studies. Memory, 25(2), 146–163. https://doi.org/10.1080/09658211.2016.1260747

Severi, C. (2012). The arts of memory: Comparative perspectives on a mental artifact. HAU: Journal of Ethnographic Theory, 2(2), 451–485. https://doi.org/10.14318/hau2.2.025

Smith, R. J., & Bryant, R. G. (1975). Metal substitutions incarbonic anhydrase: A halide ion probe study. Biochemical and Biophysical Research Communications, 66(4), 1281–1286. https://doi.org/10.1016/0006-291x(75)90498-2

Smyth, C. J., Möllby, R., & Wadström, T. (1975). Phenomenon of hot-cold hemolysis: Chelator-induced lysis of sphingomyelinase-treated erythrocytes. Infection and Immunity, 12(5), 1104–1111. https://doi.org/10.1128/iai.12.5.1104-1111.1975

Speer, M. E., & Delgado, M. R. (2017). Reminiscing about positive memories buffers acute stress responses. Nature Human Behaviour, 1(5), 0093. https://doi.org/10.1038/s41562-017-0093

Stephan, Y., Sutin, A. R., Luchetti, M., & Terracciano, A. (2020). Personality and memory performance over twenty years: Findings from three prospective studies. Journal of Psychosomatic Research, 128, 109885. https://doi.org/10.1016/j.jpsychores.2019.109885

Stopa, L., & Jenkins, A. (2007). Images of the self in social anxiety: Effects on the retrieval of autobiographical memories. Journal of Behavior Therapy and Experimental Psychiatry, 38(4), 459–473. https://doi.org/10.1016/j.jbtep.2007.08.006

Viard, A., Desgranges, B., Eustache, F., & Piolino, P. (2012). Factors affecting medial temporal lobe engagement for past and future episodic events: An ALE meta-analysis of neuroimaging studies. Brain and Cognition, 80(1), 111–125. https://doi.org/10.1016/j.bandc.2012.05.004

Witkowski, T. (2020). Elizabeth F. Loftus: Cognitive Psychology, Witness Testimony and Human Memory. In T. Witkowski, Shaping Psychology (pp. 11–27). Springer International Publishing. https://doi.org/10.1007/978-3-030-50003-0_2

Bannert, M. (2002). Managing cognitive load—Recent trends in cognitive load theory. Learning and Instruction, 12(1), 139–146. https://doi.org/10.1016/S0959-4752(01)00021-4

Ben-Shakhar, G., Bar-Hillel, M., & Lieblich, I. (1986). Trial by polygraph: Scientific and juridical issues in lie detection. Behavioral Sciences & the Law, 4(4), 459–479. https://doi.org/10.1002/bsl.2370040408

Bogaard, G., Meijer, E. H., Vrij, A., & Nahari, G. (2023). Detecting deception using comparable truth baselines. Psychology, Crime & Law,29(6),567–583. https://doi.org/10.1080/1068316X.2022.2030334

Caso, L., Palena, N., Carlessi, E., & Vrij, A. (2019). Police accuracy in truth/lie detection when judging baseline interviews. Psychiatry, Psychology and Law, 26(6), 841–850. https://doi.org/10.1080/13218719.2019.1642258

Ginton, A. (2013). A non-standard method for estimating accuracy of lie detection techniques demonstrated on a self-validating set of field polygraph examinations. Psychology, Crime & Law, 19(7), 577–594. https://doi.org/10.1080/1068316X.2012.656118

Jupe, L. M., & Keatley, D. A. (2020). Airport artificial intelligence can detect deception: Or am i lying? Security Journal, 33(4), 622–635. https://doi.org/10.1057/s41284-019-00204-7

Langleben, D. D., Dattilio, F. M., & Guthei, T. G. (2006). True Lies: Delusions and Lie-Detection Technology. The Journal of Psychiatry & Law, 34(3), 351–370. https://doi.org/10.1177/009318530603400305

Langleben, D. D., & Moriarty, J. C. (2013). Using brain imaging for lie detection: Where science, law, and policy collide. Psychology, Public Policy, and Law, 19(2), 222–234. https://doi.org/10.1037/a0028841

Malik, P., & Singh, J. (2023). Micro expression recognition—Contemporary applications and algorithms. 030018. https://doi.org/10.1063/5.0177481

McCabe, D. P., Castel, A. D., & Rhodes, M. G. (2011). The Influence of fMRI Lie Detection Evidence on Juror Decision-Making. Behavioral Sciences & the Law, 29(4), 566–577. https://doi.org/10.1002/bsl.993

Plass, J. L., Moreno, R., & Brünken, R. (Eds.). (2010). Cognitive load theory. Cambridge University Press.

Schauer, F. (2010). Neuroscience, lie-detection, and the law. Trends in Cognitive Sciences, 14(3), 101–103. https://doi.org/10.1016/j.tics.2009.12.004

Schnotz, W., & Kürschner, C. (2007). A Reconsideration of Cognitive Load Theory. Educational Psychology Review, 19(4), 469–508. https://doi.org/10.1007/s10648-007-9053-4

Sweller, J. (2011). Cognitive Load Theory. In Psychology of Learning and Motivation (Vol. 55, pp. 37–76). Elsevier. https://doi.org/10.1016/B978-0-12-387691-1.00002-8

Verigin, B. L., Meijer, E. H., & Vrij, A. (2021). A within-statement baseline comparison for detecting lies. Psychiatry, Psychology and Law, 28(1), 94–103. https://doi.org/10.1080/13218719.2020.1767712

Vrij, A. (2008). Detecting lies and deceit: Pitfalls and opportunities (2nd ed). John Wiley.

Vrij, A. (2016). Baselining as a Lie Detection Method. Applied Cognitive Psychology, 30(6), 1112–1119. https://doi.org/10.1002/acp.3288

Vrij, A., Mann, S., Leal, S., & Fisher, R. P. (2020). Combining Verbal Veracity Assessment Techniques to Distinguish Truth Tellers from Lie Tellers. The European Journal of Psychology Applied to Legal Context, 13(1), 9–19. https://doi.org/10.5093/ejpalc2021a2

Xie, H.-X., Lo, L., Shuai, H.-H., & Cheng, W.-H. (2023). An Overview of Facial Micro-Expression Analysis: Data, Methodology and Challenge. IEEE Transactions on Affective Computing, 14(3), 1857–1875. https://doi.org/10.1109/TAFFC.2022.3143100

Chira, A. M., Kirby, K., Epperlein, T., & Bräuer, J. (2023). Function predicts how people treat their dogs in a global sample. Scientific Reports, 13(1), 4954. https://doi.org/10.1038/s41598-023-31938-5

Dutton, D., & Andersson, M. (2002). Personality in Royal Pythons and the human–snake relationship. Anthrozoös, 15(3), 243–250. https://doi.org/10.2752/089279302786992531

Gosling, S. D., & Bonnenburg, A. V. (1998). An Integrative Approach to Personality Research in Anthrozoology: Ratings of Six Species of Pets and their Owners. Anthrozoös, 11(3), 148–156. https://doi.org/10.2752/089279398787000661

Gosling, S. D., Sandy, C. J., & Potter, J. (2010). Personalities of Self-Identified "Dog People" and "Cat People". Anthrozoös, 23(3), 213–222. https://doi.org/10.2752/175303710X12750451258850

Krueger, F., Mitchell, K. C., Deshpande, G., & Katz, J. S. (2021). Human–dog relationships as a working framework for exploring human–robot attachment: A multidisciplinary review. Animal Cognition, 24(2), 371–385. https://doi.org/10.1007/s10071-021-01472-w

Marchetti-Mercer, M. C. (2019). The Role of Companion Animals in the Process of Emigration: A Family Perspective. Society & Animals 28(1), 81–100. https://doi.org/10.1163/15685306-12341608

Rolph, N. C., Noble, P.-J. M., & German, A. J. (2014). How often do primary care veterinarians record the overweight status of dogs? Journal of Nutritional Science, 3, e58. https://doi.org/10.1017/jns.2014.42

Roy, M. M., & Nicholas, J. S. C. (2004). Do Dogs Resemble Their Owners? Psychological Science, 15(5), 361–363. https://doi.org/10.1111/j.0956-7976.2004.00684.x

Schöberl, I., Wedl, M., Bauer, B., Day, J., Möstl, E., & Kotrschal, K. (2012). Effects of Owner–Dog Relationship and Owner Personality on Cortisol Modulation in Human–Dog Dyads. Anthrozoös, 25(2), 199–214. https://doi.org/10.2752/175303712X13316289505422

Serpell, J. (Ed.). (2017). The domestic dog: Its evolution, behavior and interactions with people (Second edition). Cambridge University Press. Torkar, G., Fabijan, T., & Bogner, F. X. (2020).

Students' Care for Dogs, Environmental Attitudes, and Behaviour. Sustainability, 12(4), 1317. https://doi.org/10.3390/su12041317

Wells, D. L., & Hepper, P. G. (2012). The personality of "aggressive" and "non-aggressive" dog owners. Personality and Individual Differences, 53(6), 770–773. https://doi.org/10.1016/j.paid.2012.05.038
Augner, C., & Hacker, G. W. (2012). Associations between problematic mobile phone use and psychological parameters in young adults. International Journal of Public Health, 57, 437–441.

Bianchi, A., & Phillips, J. G. (2005). Psychological predictors of problem mobile phone use. Cyberpsychology & Behavior, 8(1), 39–51.

Gupta, N., Garg, S., & Arora, K. (1970). Pattern of mobile phone usage and its effects on psychological health, sleep, and academic performance in students of a medical university. National Journal of Physiology, Pharmacy and Pharmacology, 6(2), 132–132.

Hari, J. (2019). Lost connections: Why you're depressed and how to find hope. Bloomsbury Publishing Plc.
Haught, M. J., Wei, R., Xuerui, Y., & Zhang, J. (2014).

Understanding the psychology of mobile phone use and mobile shopping of the 1990s Cohort in China: A lifestyle approach. International Journal of Online Marketing (IJOM), 4(3), 68–84.

Hong, F.-Y., Chiu, S.-I., & Huang, D.-H. (2012). A model of the relationship between psychological characteristics, mobile phone addiction and use of mobile phones by Taiwanese university female students. Computers in Human Behavior, 28(6), 2152–2159.

Kleist, V. F. (2022). Stolen Focus: Why You Can't Pay Attention: By Hari, Johann, London, Bloomsbury Publishing, 2022, 340 pp.,£ 20.00 (hardcover), ISBN 978-1-5266-2022-4. Journal of Global Information Technology Management, 25(3), 254–256.

Mei, X., Hu, Z., Zhou, D., Zhou, Q., Li, X., Wang, X., & Jing, P. (2019). Sleep patterns, mobile phone use and psychological symptoms among adolescents in coastal developed city of China: An exploratory cross-sectional study. Sleep and Biological Rhythms, 17, 233–241.

Phillips, J. G., Saling, L., & Blaszczynski, A. (2008). The psychology of mobile phone use and misuse. Mobile Telephones: Networks, Applications, and Performance, 191–210.

Prentice, J. L., & Dobson, K. S. (2014). A review of the risks and benefits associated with mobile phone applications for psychological interventions. Canadian Psychology/Psychologie Canadienne, 55(4), 282.

Rachuri, K. K., Musolesi, M., Mascolo, C., Rentfrow, P. J., Longworth, C., & Aucinas, A. (2010). EmotionSense: A mobile phones based adaptive platform for experimental social psychology research. 281–290.

Reid, F. J., & Reid, D. J. (2004). Text appeal: The psychology of SMS texting and its implications for the design of mobile phone interfaces. Campus-Wide Information Systems, 21(5), 196–200.

Thomée, S. (2018). Mobile phone use and mental health. A review of the research that takes a psychological perspective on exposure. International Journal of Environmental Research and Public Health, 15(12), 2692.

Titilope, A. O. (2014). Socio-psychological dimensions of mobile phone addiction and usage patterns amongst teenagers in higher institutions of learning in Kwara State. International Journal of Information and Communication Technology Education (IJICTE), 10(2), 1–13.

Volkmer, S. A., & Lermer, E. (2019). Unhappy and addicted to your phone?–Higher mobile phone use is associated with lower well-being. Computers in Human Behavior, 93, 210–218.

Zulkefly, S. N., & Baharudin, R. (2009). Mobile phone use amongst students in a university in Malaysia: Its correlates and relationship to psychological health. European Journal of Scientific Research, 37(2), 206–218.

Bank, H. L., Robson, J., Bigelow, J. B., Morrison, J., Spell, L. H., & Kantor, R. (1981). Preparation of fingernails for trace element analysis. Clinica Chimica Acta, 116(2), 179–190. https://doi.org/10.1016/0009-8981(81)90021-8

Bhat, G., Mukhdoomi, M., Shah, B., & Ittoo, M. (2014). Dermatoglyphics: In health and disease - a review. International Journal of Research in Medical Sciences, 2(1), 31. https://doi.org/10.5455/2320-6012.ijrms20140207

Frith, H., & Heron-Allen, E. (1886). Chiromancy; Or, The Science of Palmistry: Being a Concise Exposition of the Principles and Practice of the Art of Reading the Hand by which the Past, the Present, and the Future May be Explained and Foretold. G. Routledge and Sons.

Goldin-Meadow, S. (2006). Talking and Thinking With Our Hands. Current Directions in Psychological Science, 15(1), 34–39. https://doi.org/10.1111/j.0963-7214.2006.00402.x

Grob, M., Papadopulos, N. A., Zimmermann, A., Biemer, E., & Kovacs, L. (2008). The Psychological Impact of Severe Hand Injury. Journal of Hand Surgery (European Volume), 33(3), 358–362. https://doi.org/10.1177/1753193407087026

Grunert, B. K., Smith, C. J., Devine, C. A., Fehring, B. A., Matloub, H. S., Sanger, J. R., & Yousif, N. J. (1988). Early Psychological Aspects of Severe Hand Injury. Journal of Hand Surgery, 13(2), 177–180. https://doi.org/10.1016/0266-7681_88_90132-5

Hannah, S. D. (2011). Psychosocial Issues after a Traumatic Hand Injury: Facilitating Adjustment. Journal of Hand Therapy, 24(2), 95–103. https://doi.org/10.1016/j.jht.2010.11.001

Kaneshige, T., Takagi, K., Nakamura, S., Hirasawa, T., Sada, M., & Uchida, K. (1992). Genetic analysis using fingernail DNA. Nucleic Acids Research, 20(20), 5489–5490. https://doi.org/10.1093/nar/20.20.5489

Koestler, A. J. (2010). Psychological Perspective on Hand Injury and Pain. Journal of Hand Therapy, 23(2), 199–211. https://doi.org/10.1016/j.jht.2009.09.001

Lemos, N. P., Anderson, R. A., & Robertson, J. R. (1999). Nail Analysis for Drugs of Abuse: Extraction and Determination of Cannabis in Fingernails by RIA and GC-MS. Journal of Analytical Toxicology, 23(3), 147–152. https://doi.org/10.1093/jat/23.3.147

Meier, R. J. (1980). Anthropological dermatoglyphics: A review. American Journal of Physical Anthropology, 23(S1), 147–178. https://doi.org/10.1002/ajpa.1330230509

Nardoto, G. B., Silva, S., Kendall, C., Ehleringer, J. R., Chesson, L. A., Ferraz, E. S. B., Moreira, M. Z., Ometto, J. P. H. B., & Martinelli, L. A. (2006). Geographical patterns of human diet derived from stable-isotope analysis of fingernails. American Journal of Physical Anthropology, 131(1), 137–146. https://doi.org/10.1002/ajpa.20409

261

Preuner, S., Danzer, M., Pröll, J., Pötschger, U., Lawitschka, A., Gabriel, C., & Lion, T. (2014). High-Quality DNA from Fingernails for Genetic Analysis. The Journal of Molecular Diagnostics, 16(4), 459–466. https://doi.org/10.1016/j.jmoldx.2014.02.004

Schaumann, B., & Alter, M. (1976). Dermatoglyphics in Medical Disorders. Springer Berlin Heidelberg.

Wilcox, D. E., He, X., Gui, J., Ruuge, A. E., Li, H., Williams, B. B., & Swartz, H. M. (2010). DOSIMETRY BASED ON EPR SPECTRAL ANALYSIS OF FINGERNAIL CLIPPINGS. Health Physics, 98(2), 309–317. https://doi.org/10.1097/HP.0b013e3181b27502

Wolff, C. (2016). The hand in psychological diagnosis. Routledge.

Dittmar, H. (1991). Meanings of material possessions as reflections of identity: Gender and social-marterial position in society. Journal of Social Behavior and Personality, 6(6), 165.

Dittmar, H. (1992). Perceived material wealth and first impressions. British Journal of Social Psychology, 31(4), 379–391.

Dittmar, H. (1994). Material possessions as stereotypes: Material images of different socio-economic groups. Journal of Economic Psychology, 15(4), 561–585. https://doi.org/10.1016/0167-4870(94)90011-6

Glenn, A. L., Efferson, L. M., Iyer, R., & Graham, J. (2017). Values, goals, and motivations associated with psychopathy. Journal of Social and Clinical Psychology, 36(2), 108–125.

Hawkins, M. A., & Rome, A. S. (2021). Identity relevant possessions. Journal of Strategic Marketing, 29(3), 206–226.

Holbrook, M. B. (1999). Consumer value: A framework for analysis and research. Routledge.

Kleine, S. S., & Baker, S. M. (2004). An integrative review of material possession attachment. Academy of Marketing Science Review, 1(1), 1–39.

Kleine, S. S., Iii, R. E. K., & Allen, C. T. (1995). How is a Possession 'Me' or 'Not Me'? Characterizing Types and an Antecedent of Material Possession Attachment. Journal of Consumer Research, 22(3), 327. https://doi.org/10.1086/209454

Lingenfelter, S. G. (2007). Possessions, wealth, and the cultural identities of persons: Anthropological reflections. International Bulletin of Missionary Research, 31(4), 176–182.

Pechurina, A. (2011). Russian dolls, icons, and Pushkin: Practicing cultural identity through material possessions in immigration. Laboratorium. Журнал Социальных Исследований, 3(3), 97–117.

Pechurina, A. (2020). Researching identities through material possessions: The case of diasporic objects. Current Sociology, 68(5), 669–683. https://doi.org/10.1177/0011392120927746

Weiner, A. B. (1994). Cultural difference and the density of objects. American Ethnologist, 21(2), 391–403.

Ainsworth, P. B. (2001). Offender profiling and crime analysis. Willan.
Albanese, J. S. (2000). The Causes of Organized Crime: Do Criminals Organize Around Opportunities for Crime or Do Criminal Opportunities Create New Offenders? Journal of Contemporary Criminal Justice, 16(4), 409–423. https://doi.org/10.1177/1043986200016004004

Bénézech, M., Toutin, T., Le Bihan, P., & Taguchi, H. (2006). Les composantes du crime violent: Une nouvelle méthode d'analyse comportementale de l'homicide et de sa scène. Annales Médico-psychologiques, revue psychiatrique, 164(10), 828–833. https://doi.org/10.1016/j.amp.2006.09.005

Boros, J. (2003). A bűnözői profilalkotástól a tanúkihallgatásig: Törekvések a mai kriminálpszichológiában. Magyar Pszichológiai Szemle, 58(2), 275–292. https://doi.org/10.1556/mpszle.58.2003.2.6

Canter, D. (2000). Offender profiling and criminal differentiation. Legal and Criminological Psychology, 5(1), 23–46. https://doi.org/10.1348/135532500167958

Canter, D. (2004a). Geographical Profiling of Criminals. Medico-Legal Journal, 72(2), 53–66. https://doi.org/10.1258/rsmmlj.72.2.53

Canter, D. (2004b). Offender profiling and investigative psychology. Journal of Investigative Psychology and Offender Profiling, 1(1), 1–15. https://doi.org/10.1002/jip.7

Canter, D. (2010). Offender profiling. In J. M. Brown & E. A. Campbell (Eds.), The Cambridge Handbook of Forensic Psychology (1st ed., pp. 236–241). Cambridge University Press. https://doi.org/10.1017/CBO9780511730290.030

Canter, D. V., Alison, L. J., Alison, E., & Wentink, N. (2004). The Organized/Disorganized Typology of Serial Murder: Myth or Model? Psychology, Public Policy, and Law, 10(3), 293–320. https://doi.org/10.1037/1076-8971.10.3.293

Canter, D., & Youngs, D. (2010). Investigative psychology: Offender profiling and the analysis of criminal action (Repr). Wiley.
Carson, D., & Bull, R. (Eds.). (2003). Handbook of Psychology in Legal Contexts (1st ed.). Wiley. https://doi.org/10.1002/0470013397

Charron, A., & Woodhams, J. (2010). A qualitative analysis of mock jurors' deliberations of linkage analysis evidence. Journal of Investigative Psychology and Offender Profiling, 7(2), 165–183. (n.d.).

Decker, S. H., & Curry, G. D. (2002). Gangs, gang homicides, and gang loyalty: Journal of Criminal Justice, 30(4), 343–352. https://doi.org/10.1016/S0047-2352(02)00134-4

Dowden, C., Bennell, C., & Bloomfield, S. (2007). Advances in Offender Profiling: A Systematic Review of the Profiling Literature Published Over the Past Three Decades. Journal of Police and Criminal Psychology, 22(1), 44–56. https://doi.org/10.1007/s11896-007-9000-9

Fox, B., & Farrington, D. P. (2018). What have we learned from offender profiling? A systematic review and meta-analysis of 40 years of research. Psychological Bulletin, 144(12), 1247–1274. https://doi.org/10.1037/bul0000170

Fox, B. H., & Farrington, D. P. (2012). Creating Burglary Profiles Using Latent Class Analysis: A New Approach to Offender Profiling. Criminal Justice and Behavior, 39(12), 1582–1611. https://doi.org/10.1177/0093854812457921

Gogan, D. (2008). Investigative Experience and Profile Accuracy. In R. N. Kocsis (Ed.), Criminal Profiling (pp. 383–392). Humana Press. https://doi.org/10.1007/978-1-60327-146-2_19

Häkkänen, H. (2007). Murder by Manual and Ligature Strangulation. In R. N. Kocsis (Ed.), Criminal Profiling (pp. 73–87). Humana Press. https://doi.org/10.1007/978-1-60327-146-2_4

Kocsis, R. N., Cooksey, R. W., & Irwin, H. J. (2002a). Psychological Profiling of Offender Characteristics from Crime Behaviors in Serial Rape Offences. International Journal of Offender Therapy and Comparative Criminology, 46(2), 144–169. https://doi.org/10.1177/0306624X02462003

Kocsis, R. N., Cooksey, R. W., & Irwin, H. J. (2002b). Psychological Profiling of Sexual Murders: An Empirical Model. International Journal of Offender Therapy and Comparative Criminology, 46(5), 532–554. https://doi.org/10.1177/030662402236739

Kocsis, R. N., & Palermo, G. B. (2008). Contemporary Problems in Criminal Profiling*. In R. N. Kocsis (Ed.), Criminal Profiling (pp. 327–345). Humana Press. https://doi.org/10.1007/978-1-60327-146-2_16

Kocsis, R. N., & Palermo, G. B. (2016). New Horizons: The Obstacles to Space Exploration and Disentangling Criminal Profiling. International Journal
of Offender Therapy and Comparative Criminology, 60(10), 1226–1232. https://doi.org/10.1177/0306624X15615122

Lin, L., Yu, Y., Zhang, F., Xia, K., Zhang, X., & Linhardt, R. J. (2019). Bottom-up and top-down profiling of pentosan polysulfate. The Analyst, 144(16), 4781–4786. https://doi.org/10.1039/C9AN01006H

McGuirk, N. (2021). Terrorist Profiling and Law Enforcement: Detection, Prevention, Deterrence (1st ed.). Routledge. https://doi.org/10.4324/9781003005711

Norris, G., Rafferty, E., & Campbell, J. (2010). An Examination of Content Preference in Offender Profiles. International Journal of Offender Therapy and Comparative Criminology, 54(3), 412–429. https://doi.org/10.1177/0306624X08331215

Santtila, P., Häkkänen, H., Canter, D., & Elfgren, T. (2003). Classifying homicide offenders and predicting their characteristics from crime scene behavior. Scandinavian Journal of Psychology, 44(2), 107–118. https://doi.org/10.1111/1467-9450.00328

Snook, B., Cullen, R. M., Bennell, C., Taylor, P. J., & Gendreau, P. (2008). The Criminal Profiling Illusion: What's Behind the Smoke and Mirrors? Criminal Justice and Behavior, 35(10), 1257–1276. https://doi.org/10.1177/0093854808321528

Stitt, M., Luca Borghi, G., & Arrivault, S. (2021). Targeted metabolite profiling as a top-down approach to uncover interspecies diversity and identify key conserved operational features in the Calvin–Benson cycle. Journal of Experimental Botany, 72(17), 5961–5986. https://doi.org/10.1093/jxb/erab291

Taylor, S., Lambeth, D., Green, G., Bone, R., & Cahillane, M. A. (2012). Cluster Analysis Examination of Serial Killer Profiling Categories: A Bottom-Up Approach. Journal of Investigative Psychology and Offender Profiling, 9(1), 30–51. https://doi.org/10.1002/jip.149

Williams, T. J., Picano, J. J., Roland, R. R., & Banks, L. M. (2006). Introduction to Operational Psychology. In C. H. Kennedy & E. A. Zillmer (Eds.), Military psychology: Clinical and operational applications (pp. 193–214). The Guilford Press. (n.d.).

Wood, J. L. (Ed.). (2013). Crime and crime reduction: The importance of group processes. Routledge.
Woodworth, M., & Porter, S. (2000). [No title found]. Expert Evidence, 7(4), 241–264. https://doi.org/10.1023/A:1016655103536

Bodziak, W. J. (2017). Forensic footwear evidence: Detection, recovery and examination. CRC Press.

Bodziak, W. J., Hammer, L., Johnson, G. M., & Schenck, R. (2012). Determining the significance of outsole wear characteristics during the forensic examination of footwear impression evidence. Journal of Forensic Identification, 62(3), 254–278.

Hilderbrand, D. S. (2007). Footwear, the missed evidence. Staggs Pub.

Kerstholt, J. H., Paashuis, R., & Sjerps, M. (2007). Shoe print examinations: Effects of expectation, complexity and experience. Forensic Science International, 165(1), 30–34.

Koehler, J. J. (2011). If the shoe fits they might acquit: The value of forensic science testimony. Journal of Empirical Legal Studies, 8, 21–48.

Morgan, R. M., Freudiger-Bonzon, J., Nichols, K. H., Jellis, T., Dunkerley, S., Zelazowski, P., & Bull, P. A. (2009). The forensic analysis of sediments recovered from footwear. Criminal and Environmental Soil Forensics, 253–269.

Naples, V. L., & Miller, J. S. (2004). Making tracks: The forensic analysis of footprints and footwear impressions. The Anatomical Record Part B: The New Anatomist: An Official Publication of the American Association of Anatomists, 279(1), 9–15.

Rida, I., Fei, L., Proença, H., Nait-Ali, A., & Hadid, A. (2019). Forensic shoe-print identification: A brief survey. arXiv Preprint arXiv:1901.01431.

Skerrett, J., Neumann, C., & Mateos-Garcia, I. (2011). A Bayesian approach for interpreting shoemark evidence in forensic casework: Accounting for wear features. Forensic Science International, 210(1–3), 26–30.

Srihari, S. N. (2011). Analysis of footwear impression evidence. US DoJ Report.

Vernon, W. (2006). The development and practice of forensic podiatry. Journal of Clinical Forensic Medicine, 13(6–8), 284–287.

Zhang, L., & Allinson, N. (2005). Automatic shoeprint retrieval system for use in forensic investigations. 99, 137–142.

Bell, S. (1999). Tattooed: A Participant Observer's Exploration of Meaning. Journal of American Culture, 22(2), 53–58. https://doi.org/10.1111/j.1542-734X.1999.2202_53.x

Buss, L., & Hodges, K. (2017). Marked: Tattoo as an Expression of Psyche. Psychological Perspectives, 60(1), 4–38. https://doi.org/10.1080/00332925.2017.1282251

De Andrade, A. M. (2015). Recovering the psychic apparatus. The International Journal of Psychoanalysis, 96(3), 521–533. https://doi.org/10.1111/1745-8315.12355

Green, T. (2009). The Tattoo Encyclopedia: A guide to choosing your tattoo. Simon and Schuster.
Hultberg, B., Lundblad, A., Masson, P. K., & Ockerman, P. A. (1975).

Karacaoglan, U. (2012). Tattoo and taboo: On the meaning of tattoos in the analytic process. The International Journal of Psychoanalysis, 93(1), 5–28. https://doi.org/10.1111/j.1745-8315.2011.00497.x

Kertzman, S., Kagan, A., Hegedish, O., Lapidus, R., & Weizman, A. (2019). Do young women with tattoos have lower self-esteem and body image than their peers without tattoos? A non-verbal repertory grid technique approach. PLOS ONE, 14(1), e0206411. https://doi.org/10.1371/journal.pone.0206411

Kıvanç Altunay, İ., Mercan, S., & Özkur, E. (2021). Tattoos in Psychodermatology. Psych, 3(3), 269–278. https://doi.org/10.3390/psych3030021

Kosut, M. (2000). Tattoo Narratives: The intersection of the body, self-identity and society. Visual Sociology, 15(1), 79–100. https://doi.org/10.1080/14725860008583817

Madfis, E., & Arford, T. (2013). The dilemmas of embodied symbolic representation: Regret in contemporary American tattoo narratives. The Social Science Journal, 50(4), 547–556. https://doi.org/10.1016/j.soscij.2013.07.012

Mun, J. M., Janigo, K. A., & Johnson, K. K. (2012). Tattoo and the self. Clothing and Textiles Research Journal, 30(2), 134–148.

Namir, S. (2006). Embodiments and Disembodiments: The Relation of Body Modifications to Two Psychoanalytic Treatments. Psychoanalysis, Culture & Society, 11(2), 217–223. https://doi.org/10.1057/palgrave.pcs.2100085

Roggenkamp, H., Nicholls, A., & Pierre, J. M. (2017). Tattoos as a window to the psyche: How talking about skin art can inform psychiatric practice. World Journal of Psychiatry, 7(3), 148–158. https://doi.org/10.5498/wjp.v7.i3.148

Snell, D., & Hodgetts, D. (2007). Heavy Metal, identity and the social negotiation of a community of practice. Journal of Community &

272

Applied Social Psychology, 17(6), 430–445. https://doi.org/10.1002/casp.943

Sundberg, K., & Kjellman, U. (2018). The tattoo as a document. Journal of Documentation, 74(1), 18–35. https://doi.org/10.1108/JD-03-2017-0043

Weidner, K., Bal, A., Rains, S., & Leeds, C. (2016). Tattooing and brand sponsorship: How far is too far? Journal of Product & Brand Management, 25(4), 387–393. https://doi.org/10.1108/JPBM-09-2015-0977

Witkoś, J., & Hartman-Petrycka, M. (2020). Gender Differences in Subjective Pain Perception during and after Tattooing. International Journal of Environmental Research and Public Health, 17(24), 9466. https://doi.org/10.3390/ijerph17249466

Riddle answer - He would use the shovel to make a pile of dirt to climb up to the window and jump out.

Printed in the USA
CPSIA information can be obtained
at www.ICGtesting.com
LVHW021015230524
781199LV00007B/170